07

P9-EGM-218

The *Carpetbagger's* *Children*

&

The *Actor*

ALSO BY HORTON FOOTE

The Last of the Thorntons
Beginnings: A Memoir
To Kill a Mockingbird, Tender Mercies, and
    The Trip to Bountiful: Three Screenplays
Farewell: A Memoir of a Texas Childhood
Courtship, Valentine's Day, 1918: Three Plays
    from the Orphans' Home Cycle
Collected Plays

812 F688C FOOTE
Foote, Horton.
The carpetbagger's children

JAN 2 3 2006

The *Carpetbagger's Children*

&

The *Actor*

2 plays

Horton Foote

SEWANEE WRITERS' SERIES / THE OVERLOOK PRESS

CAUTION: Professionals and amateurs are hereby warned that performance of THE CARPET-BAGGER'S CHILDREN and THE ACTOR is subject to a royalty. They are fully protected under the copyright laws of the United States of America, and of all countries covered by the International Copyright Union, including the Dominion of Canada and the rest of the Pan-American Copyright Convention and the Universal Copyright Convention, the Berne Convention, and of all countries with which the United States has reciprocal copyright relations. All rights, including professional/amateur stage performing, motion picture, recitation, lecturing, public reading, radio broadcasting, television, video or sound taping, all other forms of mechanical or electronic reproduction, such as CD-ROM, CD-I, DVD, information storage and retrieval systems and photocopying, and the rights of translation into foreign languages, are strictly reserved. Particular emphasis is placed upon the matter of readings, permission for which must be secured from the author's agent in writing.

The stage performance rights in THE CARPETBAGGER'S CHILDREN and THE ACTOR (other than first class rights) are controlled exclusively by DRAMATAISTS PLAY SERVICE, INC., 440 Park Avenue South, New York, NY 10016. No professional or nonprofessional performance of the Plays (excluding first class professional performance) may be given with obtaining in advance written permission of DRAMATAISTS PLAY SERVICE, INC., and paying the requisite fee.

Inquiries concerning all other rights should be addressed to The Gersh Agency, 130 West 42nd Street, New York, NY 10036. Attn: Peter Hagen.

First published in the United States in 2003 by
The Overlook Press, Peter Mayer Publishers, Inc.
Woodstock & New York

WOODSTOCK:
One Overlook Drive
Woodstock, NY 12498
www.overlookpress.com
[for individual orders, bulk and special sales, contact our Woodstock office]

NEW YORK:
141 Wooster Street
New York, NY 10012

Copyright © 2003 by Horton Foote

All Rights Reserved. No part of this publication may be reproduced or transmitted in any form or by any means, electronic or mechanical, including photocopy, recording, or any information storage and retrieval system now known or to be invented without permission in writing from the publisher, except by a reviewer who wishes to quote brief passages in connection with a review written for inclusion in a magazine, newspaper, or broadcast.

Library of Congress Cataloging-in-Publication Data

Foote, Horton.
The carpetbagger's children ; &, The actor : two plays / by Horton Foote.
p. cm.
1. Fathers and daughters—Drama. 2. Fathers—Death—Drama.
3. Young men—Drama. 4. Actors—Drama. 5. Texas—Drama.
I. Foote, Horton. Actor. II. Title: Actor. III. Title.

PS3511.O344C37 2003   812'.54—dc21   2003040574

Book design and type formatting by Bernard Schleifer
Manufactured in the United States of America
FIRST EDITION
1 2 3 4 5 6 7 8 9 10
ISBN 1-58567-297-1

In memory of my wife, Lillian

The *Carpetbagger's Children*

The world premiere of *The Carpetbagger's Children* was presented at the Alley Theatre, Gregory Boyd, artistic director, and Paul Tetreault, managing director, on June 6, 2001, directed by Michael Wilson.

Cast

CORNELIA	*Roberta Maxwell*
GRACE ANN	*Jean Stapleton*
SISSIE	*Hallie Foote*

The scenic design was by Jeff Cowie, the costume design was by David Woolard, the lighting design was by Rui Rita, the sound design and original music were by John Gromada, the stage manager was Amy Knotts, and the casting was by Cindy Tolan.

The Carpetbagger's Children was presented by the Lincoln Center Theater under the direction of André Bishop and Bernard Gersten, and opened at the Mitzi E. Newhouse Theater on March 25, 2002.

The stage is in darkness. The lights are slowly brought up. At three cor-
ners of the stage are chairs. In each chair sits one of the Thompson girls:
CORNELIA, GRACE ANNE, *and* SISSIE. CORNELIA *is looking at a ledger*
book and writing figures, GRACE ANNE *is sewing, and* SISSIE *sits in si-*
lence. In the center of the stage is a table with many family pictures on
it and four chairs placed around it. In the distance we hear dance music.
As the lights are brought up on CORNELIA'*s area she is going over ac-*
counts in the ledger book.

CORNELIA

Hear that music? That is from the Opera House. They're having a dance there tonight. Whenever I hear dance music I
think of Beth. She loved to dance. I never learned to dance.
Grace Anne danced and Sissie, but Beth was the loveliest
dancer I ever saw. Beth was Papa's favorite when she was
alive, no question about that. Mama's too. Mine. Brother's. We
all adored her. She went away one winter to visit some cousins
in Saint Louis and stayed seven months. We missed her so.
Let her stay as long as she wants, Papa said, she's having a
good time. She deserves it. We were such a happy family then
it seemed to me. Papa's closest friend was Colonel Hawkins.
He lived next door and had been captain in the Confederate
Army. Beth used to say, Look the war is over for sure now,
here comes Papa and Colonel Hawkins walking home together
again, talking away. They'd walk up to the sidewalk leading to

our house. Stop and talk and talk and talk. Until Mrs. Hawkins
would send one of her girls out with some excuse to get
Colonel Hawkins into the house because she couldn't stand
that Colonel Hawkins and Papa were best friends. You see
Mrs. Hawkins was doing all she could to keep the Confederacy alive here. And the Colonel still had a plantation not five
miles out from Harrison. And Papa, well, much to my shame
when I was growing up, had come to Texas with the Union
Army and had liked what he saw so much that he decided to
come on back here after the war to live. Anyway, that's the
story we were brought up on. However it was, when he got
here again things were in chaos, the slaves were all freed, and
the plantation owners couldn't hold onto their land, and, according to Papa, Colonel Hawkins was about to lose his plantation, and Papa, being one of the few white Republicans here
then, had been appointed county treasurer and tax collector
which enabled him to know first on who couldn't pay their
taxes. There was another white man in the courthouse called
Jenkins. Before the war began he was elected county judge
and was serving when the issue of secession came up in Texas,
and every official in the courthouse voted for secession except
Jenkins. He voted against it, and his vote made him so un-
popular he had to leave in the dark of night and flee to Mex-
ico. He stayed there during the war, but as soon as Texas sur-
rendered and asked to be let back in the Union he returned
and was reinstated as county judge and he came to Papa and
said, I hear Colonel Hawkins can't pay his taxes and may have
to give up his land. I want you to find a way to raise the taxes
on his land so he won't for sure be able to pay them, so I can
get hold of it. Papa refused and went to Colonel Hawkins and
told him what was going on and Colonel Hawkins got together
with some of his friends and called on Jenkins that night and
told him if he stayed in town another day he would be killed.
That frightened Jenkins and he left town for good. Colonel
Hawkins was able to pay his taxes, and that year he made a
wonderful cotton crop, and he decided to move his family off
the plantation and into town and bought a vacant lot next to
us and built his house. I don't know whether it was his friend-

ship or something in Papa's character that made people here forgive Papa for being in the Union Army, a Republican, and a carpetbagger. Grace Anne said they never did forgive him, they tolerated him because of his friendship with Colonel Hawkins. But that's Grace Anne for you. She always had to be different from the rest of us. I think she always resented the fact that Beth was Papa's favorite. Mama's too. Mine. Everybody's. But then Grace Anne was not pretty. Not plain exactly, but not ever pretty. Sissie wasn't really a beauty either, but she was always so sweet, had the disposition of a saint, born that way, that you didn't really care what she looked like. But Beth was beautiful. And that wasn't just my opinion. Everybody in town thought so. She was beautiful and she was stylish. That was another problem Grace Anne had. She wasn't stylish. How do you define stylish? I wish I knew, but I know when someone is stylish and when they aren't. Grace Anne could wear the exact same dress as Beth and it wouldn't mean anything at all. Let Beth put it on and my goodness she'd just dazzle you. And Beth was the Big Boss of the family too, you know. Even Papa asked her opinion about things. And then she got sick. We called in all the doctors here, Dr. Valls and Dr. Andrews and Dr. Davidson, and they all examined her and consulted among themselves and said they didn't know what was wrong and Papa had better take her to a specialist, and so I went with him and we took her to New Orleans and Papa spent a fortune on doctors and whatever it was, we never really understood. They said it couldn't be cured and we were going to lose her, and Papa thanked them and said I'll take her home then, and Beth thought she was cured and that's why she was going home and we didn't tell her anything different, but she couldn't understand why if she was cured and able to go home she couldn't walk and had to stay on her berth all the way home. Colonel Hawkins had arranged for a number of the men in town to meet our train and they carried Beth off the train to a wagon they had waiting for her and lifted her onto the wagon, and Papa said to me, Look they have covered the streets with straw so she will have a smooth ride to our house, and because of the straw there were no ruts to jar the

wagon as we took her home. The men carried her up the stairs
to her room, and the street in front of our house was covered
with straw every day the whole time she was sick, so that the
wagons and the horses passing the house went by as silently as
humanly possible. And we all prayed day and night for God to
make her well, Grace Anne praying the loudest of all. I could
hear her praying in the next room to mine. Dear God, take
me, but spare our dear sister Beth. But none of our prayers
did any good and she died three weeks after we brought her
home thinking all the time she was going to get well. She died
at two o'clock in the morning. Papa was sitting up with her
bathing her face with a cold cloth and I heard him sob and I
went to him and he was holding her sobbing. We've lost Beth,
he said over and over. We've lost Beth. A week after her funeral Papa called me into his room and asked me to shut the
door and I did and he said, Cornelia, I'm turning to you now
that Beth is gone. Your brother means well, but he hasn't a lot
of common sense, nor does Grace Anne or Sissie, sweet and
lovable all of them in their own way and I feel blessed in having them, but I don't think any of them are ready for any kind
of responsibility. And so now that Beth is gone I'm turning to
you, so if anything happens to me you will know what to do.
And beginning tomorrow I will take you each day to one of the
farms and tell you what I paid for it and what it's worth now
and who are good and responsible tenants and who's not. And
he did. Every afternoon for a month he would come home
early, hitch up the buggy and off we'd go. Brother and Sissie
would go along sometimes too, but never Grace Anne. He
would ask her, but she would always pretend she had something else to do. Slipping off and seeing Jackson Le Grand we
found out later. At night Papa would go over his books with
me. What the taxes on the land were, what arrangements he
had with this tenant and what arrangements he had with that
tenant. And one night he said to me, Cornelia, I'm concerned
about your brother. I worry if he doesn't have something to do,
something to give him a sense of responsibility, he'll never
amount to anything. Snyder's Dry Good Store is up for sale
and I'm thinking of buying it for your brother. What do you

think of that idea? I said I thought it was a good one, and that's what Papa did. Bought Mr. Snyder's Dry Good Store and put Brother in charge. And at first it all went well. Then Mr. Snyder did a sneaky thing and opened another store just down the street and took away most of Brother's customers. We heard from friends that he was referring to Brother's store as the carpetbagger's store, but when Papa went to him about that he denied he ever said it.

(*The music is heard again.*)

Beth told me once when she was so sick, When I get out of this bed I'm going to teach you to dance, but of course she never got well and I never learned.

She goes back to her ledger book as the lights fade and are brought up left on GRACE ANNE *seated in a rocker sewing on a dress.*

GRACE ANNE

Poor Brother. Papa bought a dry goods store for him, a chicken hatchery, a Studebaker car dealership, and they all failed. And he worked hard too, didn't drink, was responsible and tended to business, but he didn't prosper. Someone said to me once, Grace Anne, nothing your brother touches prospers does it? And it certainly seemed that way. So after Papa died he just gave up and quit trying. Stayed home all the time. Cornelia pretended he was helping her, and he would ride out to the farms with her and inspect the crops, but she never let him near the books or write out a single check. I knew that for a fact because once when Brother got mad at her he came over to my house complaining but I said, What can I do, Brother? I have no authority at all. Lost that the day I married. Oh, I knew about Brother and his mistress, that mulatto woman Hessie Gallagher. She made the dress I'm wearing right now. Yes. She did. It's almost fifteen years old this dress and she made it. She was the best dressmaker I've ever known and the town has ever known. She lived across the tracks just two blocks behind the icehouse, and I want you to know she lived in a nice house, always freshly painted, neat yard, lovely flowers. All you needed to do was to get to T. Gordon's or Schwartz's store and pick out a pattern you liked and take it to

Hessie and say, Hessie, can you have this for me in a week, and she'd say, Yes, ma'am, and she'd have it for you too. And when she died last year I went to her funeral with five friends of mine, all customers of hers. We were the only white people there. I don't know why Brother gave her up. I never could figure if Hessie knew either, but whatever it was, it didn't seem to affect her one way or the other, for we'd always greet each other the same and spend a few minutes talking about the weather and the price of things, and then I'd show her my patterns and sometimes she'd suggest a few improvements or sometimes she'd say, I think you should keep it just as it is. Once in a while, after Papa died, I would go see Mama. And Mama by this time had started getting all mixed up in her mind, and every time I'd go over to see her, which was at the most every two months or so, she'd start hollering to the help or my sisters or anyone around at the time, Get her out of here, I know what she's come for. She's trying to trap Brother into marrying her, just like the rest of the women in this town. I'm on to them. They come over here you know and I say, What do you want? And they say, We're here to play bridge with Sissie or Cornelia, and I say, Like hell you are. Like hell you are. You're not here to play bridge with nobody. You're here after Brother. And my sisters would say, Mama, do you know who that is? That's Grace Anne. Your daughter Grace Anne and she has come to see you, and I wanted to say, Mama, you're wasting your breath because Brother has never been interested in white women. That was before Mrs. Carpenter of course. Once he started going with her they were inseparable. He could take her everyplace because she was white. The only place he couldn't take her was his own house, because Mama would have a fit when she'd see them together and start screaming, Get that hussy out of here, she is trying to trap Brother, and poor Mrs. Carpenter would have to leave. Well, I have to make my own dresses now. I couldn't afford Hessie now if she were alive. If my luck doesn't change soon I may have to start sewing for other people too. How come my brother and sisters are rich and I'm not? Well, that's a long story. They never made any more money than I did. Papa

made it all, made it in a hurry too, my friends used to whisper
to me. You see Papa was a Union soldier sent to Texas and
when the war was over he liked it so well around here he decided to come on back. Anyway, that's Mama's story. People in
town have another story which I was told often enough by so-
called friends in school. He was sent here as a part of the Reconstruction when the Yankees took over the county and the
courthouse, and he got himself appointed county treasurer
and tax collector, and when the plantations were breaking up
and people couldn't pay their taxes, he grabbed land right and
left and held onto it. When I was growing up I always waited
for the day in school when the Civil War would come up and
somebody would point to me and say, as if it had never been
said before, Her papa was a carpetbagger. Anyway, like Mama
once said, money stopped that kind of talk once it had been
established Papa was a rich carpetbagger and nobody was ever
going to take the land or his money away from him. The one
thing I remember most about my papa was calling us to him
just before we said our prayers and making us promise we
would never ever sell or divide a piece of the land he had gotten together. And everybody kept that promise too, everybody
except me. And they've never in their hearts forgiven me for
that, and I don't think they ever will. Mama and Papa never
wanted us to marry, you know. None of us. Not only Brother
but none of us girls. They thought everybody was after our
land and our money. Well I defied them and eloped with Jackson Le Grand and when Papa heard what I'd done, he and
Brother were after us to stop us, but we'd taken the train to
Victoria and got married there in the parlor of a cousin of
Jackson's, so by the time Brother and Papa found out where
we were it was too late to stop us. He sent word to where we
were honeymooning not to bother ever to come home again
with or without my husband, and I never did while Papa was
alive. When Papa died I asked Jackson if he'd go with me to
the funeral and he said, No, he didn't want me around when
he was alive and I've no interest in going now he's dead. So I
wrote Mama a note saying I would like to come and say goodbye to Papa and it was Cornelia that called me on the phone

and said I could come, but without Jackson, so I went to the
house, to the church, and to the cemetery, sat with the family
at the church and at the cemetery, and when it was all over I
asked if I could go back to the house with them and they said
yes. Brother and I weren't speaking by then. He'd made a re-
mark about Jackson uptown the day after Papa died that was
repeated to me and I called him up and I said, Brother, did
you say uptown yesterday that Jackson had married me for my
money? Yes, I did, he said, because I think it's true. So does
everybody else in town. What money? I said. I don't have a
dime to my name and you know it. But he's counting on the
future. What future? I asked. The day Mama dies and the estate is divided. That's a lie and you know it, I said. Jackson
married me for love and nothing else. I bet, he said. Well, you
can just march back downtown, I said, and tell everyone you
have told that lie to that it's a lie, or I'll never speak to you
again. Suit yourself, he said, suit yourself. When I told Jackson later on what Brother said, he said, Well, you will be rich
one day. There's nothing wrong with that. Just be sure you're
smart and look out for what is coming to you, because your
papa's gone now and Beth and so there's only Sissie and Cornelia and Brother and your mama. I know when your mama
goes. What are you talking about? I said. When Mama goes?
When she dies. Your papa left everything in her name, when
she dies who is she leaving it to? I don't think she's leaving it
to anybody. I just think the estate will be kept together and we
will live off the proceeds. Who will? We all will, I said. Are you
getting any of it now? he asked. No, I had to admit. And I
don't want any of it as long as Brother and I are not speaking
and you're not allowed to come to the house. And I was happy
too, married to Jackson. From the very start we were happy.
There was one rough time for us when our first baby died and
I was told I couldn't have any more children. I sent for Mama
then and asked her to please come and see me as I knew Papa
would never allow me to come to the house to see her and I
needed comforting. And she defied Papa for once in her life
and came to where we were living and even spoke to Jackson.
She sent me a check a week later, she said to help with the fu-

neral expenses incurred at the time of the death of the baby. Then to the surprise of the doctor I got pregnant again and had Lily Beth and Dolores Susan. Those days Jackson had a job at the cotton gin. Making very little, I might add. Then Mr. Carson who ran the cotton gin replaced him with his son, and there were no other jobs in sight just then, and Jackson said to me one day after Papa died, You know I think I'll try farming. I think I could make a go of that. What are you going to farm? I asked. Well, honey, he said, you know you'll one day have a share of a very large estate. Some said uptown yesterday your mama was left twenty thousand acres by your papa. Now your share will be, when it's divided, at least five thousand acres. When will that be? I said. When your mama dies. Don't talk about Mama dying, I said. She could live a long, long time. She could, he said. She could. And it turned out I was right. She did live a long, long time.

She goes back to her sewing as the lights fade from her and then are brought up on SISSIE'*s area.* SISSIE *sings "Mighty Lak a Rose." The songs that are heard during the play are sometimes to be prerecorded and sometimes sung live. When* SISSIE *finishes singing she turns to the audience.*

SISSIE

I'm the baby. I always liked being the baby. I liked being told what to do and what not to do, what to think and what not to think. My daughter got mad at me once and said, Sissie—she always called me Sissie, never Mama—Sissie I don't think you have ever had a thought or an opinion of your own. Ever. I expect that's right. When Grace Anne married Jackson Le Grand I thought to myself I could never do anything like that. Never upset Papa or Mama or my sister like that. I had such a happy childhood. Roberta Thatcher was my best friend and lived just down the street and whenever it rained, and it rained a lot, Roberta would bring her paper dolls over here and we would play paper dolls all day up in our attic. I had a cousin too, Lenora, who would come over and play with me. But she had such a sad life, so different from mine. She married Leon Davis just out of high school, and her papa and mama left here and moved to Houston and she and Mr. Davis went soon after.

We didn't stay in touch much but I knew things weren't going well for them, because her papa, my Uncle Joe, Mama's brother, came twice to try and borrow money from Cornelia, and Cornelia felt she had to say no. And then there was some property Mama was left that Uncle Joe said he should have a share of and he sued Mama about that but he lost, and then Uncle Joe stopped speaking to us. The next thing we heard was that Lenora had left Leon and taken their three children and had moved in with her mama and papa and then we read in the Houston paper that Leon had shot Uncle Joe, in self defense he told the reporters, because Uncle Joe had tried to stab him with a butcher knife. Which I didn't believe because I always thought Uncle Joe was kind and gentle, but I kept my opinion to myself since the rest of the family was still mad at Uncle Joe for suing us. Anyway, where was I?

(*In the distance we hear a child faintly singing*
"Jesus Loves Me." It should be prerecorded.)

Oh yes. About playing paper dolls on rainy afternoons. It was about that time I found out I had a sweet singing voice. Mrs. Payne at Sunday school heard me singing.

(SISSIE *joins in singing with the recording of the*
child singing "Jesus Loves Me.")

And she called up Mama and said, Sissie has a sweet singing voice and I'd love to have her study singing with me, and Mama asked me if I wanted to and I said, Yes, as long as I don't have to sing before anyone, because I would be terrified to stand up in the choir like Miss Agnes Treat and sing a solo, and Mama said, No one will ever make you do that if you don't want to, so I went once a week and studied singing, and finally I got so I could sing before Papa and Mama and Brother and Cornelia at the house. Papa's favorites were "Just a Song at Twilight" and "After the Ball." And pretty soon I got to singing around town. I sang at the Methodist Washington Birthday Tea three years in a row, and I sang "Oh, Promise Me" at Judy Gaylord's wedding, and I was going to sing "The Broken Link" at Hester Galbraith's funeral, but I became so emotional looking at her coffin while I was singing that I began to sob and cry in the middle of the song and Cornelia had to come and

THE CARPETBAGGER'S CHILDREN   21

lead me out of the church. No one ever asked me to sing at a
funeral after that. It was about that time I met Ralph Goodman. He asked if he could call on me and I asked Cornelia
what she thought and she talked it over with Mama, and
Mama said it would be all right as long as he didn't try to take
me for a walk or to the picture show, and so he came over one
Sunday night after church and he asked if we had a Victrola
and I said we did and he said, Do you think your mama would
mind if we danced? And I said, Have you forgotten this is
Sunday? We don't dance here in this house on Sunday, and he
said, Oh, forgive me, I forgot. I was so taken with you I forgot what day it is. Well, he kept coming over and Mama gave
us permission to dance as long as she or Cornelia were in the
room and one night he told me he loved me and would I
marry him? And I began to cry then and he said, What's the
matter? And I said, I can't marry you, and he said, Why not,
don't you like me? And I said, I do, and he said, I love you,
do you think you could ever love me? And I said, I don't know.
Maybe. And he said, If you found out one day you loved me
would you marry me then? And I said, No, and he said, Why
not? And I said, Well, because of what Grace Anne did. She
eloped with Jackson Le Grand and Papa never spoke to her
again. And he said he wasn't talking about eloping, he wanted
to get married in a church before God, and I said, Mama
wouldn't ever say yes to that because Papa didn't want any of
us ever to marry, and he said, Let me ask and see what she
says to me, because I'm not Jackson Le Grand. I'm a go-get-
ter and I'm going to get a fine job in Houston, which I can't
discuss yet, and I want to take you with me. Oh, I couldn't do
that, I said, I'd miss my family living in Houston, and he said,
Just give it a try and if you don't like Houston we'll come back
here. And can we live here with Mama? I asked. Oh, I don't
think that would be practical, he said, but we could live near
them, and Mama came in then and he said, May I speak to
you about a very serious matter? And she said yes and they
went into the next room and he asked if we could marry and
she called in Cornelia and Brother and asked their opinion
and Cornelia said it was all right with her as long as Ralph

Goodman would sign a paper never asking that the estate be
divided as that was the wish of Papa and he said he had no interest in the estate, and they called me in then and told me I
could get married, and we got married in the Methodist
Church, and I asked Grace Anne to be my matron of honor
but she refused as she said she'd had to elope and not been
spoken to for a number of years after that. Anyway, it was a
lovely wedding and I moved to Houston, but I missed my
family so that Ralph said I could come back here and live with
Mama and he would come out every other weekend to be
with me as his job in Houston was too important to leave, and
that's what I did and that's what he does. He comes out every
other weekend. And so I keep happy and whenever I get discouraged I just sing to myself one of the songs I used to sing
in Sunday school.

(SISSIE *sings live "Brighten the Corner Where You Are" as she is seated in
her chair and the lights on her fade and are brought up on* CORNELIA's
area.)

CORNELIA

I wasn't with Papa when he died, I'm sorry to say. Colonel
Hawkins had died the year before and Papa, I believe, never
got over missing him. He stopped walking to town soon after
Colonel Hawkins died and closed his office in town and
moved his office to our house. Papa was talking about Beth all
the time then. She would have been almost forty if she had
lived. And he worried about Grace Anne, although he still
wouldn't speak to her, and had me inquire from friends of hers
how they were getting along. By the hardest, I was told. When
Papa heard that he said, Let's start giving Grace Anne, not a
penny for her husband, but Grace Anne a hundred dollars a
month as her share of the profits from the estate, that way I'll
know she won't starve. He sent me over to talk to her and take
a check, but she refused the help. Well, we tried, he said. I'll
live to see the day she'll be coming here begging for help. But
he never did, of course, he died before that ever happened.
He wasn't sick at all, you know. He and I had been out to one
of the farms to see how the crops looked and when we came

home he went into the parlor and called Sissie to come and sing for him. And Sissie asked if she could call her friend Roberta Thatcher to accompany her on the piano and Papa said, No, just sing all by yourself. Mama and Brother joined us then. And she sang five songs for him and then he said would she sing "Marching through Georgia." And she said she didn't want to sing that, and he said, Why not? And she said, Because Sherman was vile and a beast and did terrible things to the South, and he said, Who told you that? And she said, I heard it at the meeting of the United Daughters of the Confederacy and he said, Do you go to the United Daughters of the Confederacy? And she said, I only went once with my friend Roberta Thatcher. And he turned to Mama and said, Do you know about this? And Mama said, No, it's the first I've heard about it, and Sissie began crying then and said she was sorry and would never go again and Papa said she was forgiven and for Sissie to stop crying, and she said she would, and she sang "Marching through Georgia" then, and I felt ashamed of myself but I was hoping none of our friends would come in just then, because I knew how all of them felt about Sherman, and Papa said when she finished that to show how broad-minded he was he would like her to sing "Dixie" and she did and we all joined in singing it with her, including Papa and Brother, and then Sissie started crying again and when Papa asked her what the matter was she said she missed our sister Beth and we all started crying then, even Papa and Brother, and Mama went and got Beth's picture, which none of us felt did her justice but it was the only picture we had. The next morning Papa called me into his office and said he wanted to let me look at his will which he had just drawn up and I read it and saw that the estate was going to be left to Mama, under certain conditions, that it was to never be divided under any circumstances and that proceeds from the estate were to be divided equally to each of us including Grace Anne and I was always to be in charge of the estate. Mama asked us to dinner then, and Papa told me to go on without him, he was tired and thought he would take a nap and then he asked me to have Sissie come into his room and sing to him, as her singing

soothed him, and she went in and we could hear her singing,
"O, the Clanging Bells of Time."

(*We hear* CORNELIA's *memory of* SISSIE *singing
"O, the Clanging Bells of Time." It should be prerecorded.*)

"O, the clanging bells of time, Night and day they never cease;
We are wearied with their chime, For they do not bring us
peace; And we hush our breath to hear, And we strain our eyes
to see—" And then her screaming, screaming like I've never
heard anyone scream before, and we all went running up the
stairs to Papa's bedroom and Sissie was beside his bed screaming, not singing anymore, just screaming, and I looked at Papa
on the bed and I said, My God, Mama, Papa is dead, and she
began to scream then and the cook heard us screaming and
came up to see what the matter was and she saw Papa dead
and she started to scream too. Brother went right away for
Doctor Valls and I was trying to comfort Mama and Sissie and
Louisa, the cook, when Brother came in with Dr. Valls and
when I saw Dr. Valls I began to cry and Brother began to cry
too and Dr. Valls looked at Papa and said, You're right, son, he
is dead, I'm sorry to say, and the town has lost a fine man.
Well, I got hold of myself then and said to Brother, Go to Mr.
Ross's funeral home and have him come for Papa. When
would you like the funeral? Brother said, and I said, Heavens
that depends on so much. Like what? he said. Well, what if
Papa's cousins that live in Saint Louis, that Beth spent seven
months with, want to come? How long would it take them to
get here? It turned out they couldn't come, sent a lovely wire
of condolences and flowers. And everybody in town was so
nice. I never saw so much food as was sent over. Even Mrs.
Hawkins sent food and flowers. Anyway, in the late afternoon
of the day Papa died Brother went to the post office and came
home with a letter to Mama from Grace Anne wanting to
come to the funeral and we talked it over and Mama told me
to call her and say she was welcome to come without Jackson.
Which I did and she thanked me and said she would be with
us and to give her love to Mama. And she told someone later
that Jackson wouldn't have come even if he had been asked, as

he was very resentful still at the treatment shown him by Papa. Anyway, she came and we made her welcome and it was my duty after the funeral to ask her up to Papa's office and explain to her about the will and that she was to share in whatever the estate made after certain expenses were deducted and she said,

GRACE ANNE
(*Speaking from her chair*)
What expenses?

CORNELIA
Well, I was to get a salary as I had for some time.

GRACE ANNE
For what?

CORNELIA
I was going to manage the estate and Papa specified in his will that I was going to be paid for that.

GRACE ANNE
(*Getting up from her chair*)
How much?

CORNELIA
Two hundred dollars a month.

GRACE ANNE
Mercy, that's a fortune. Why that's more than Jackson Le Grand makes at the cotton gin keeping their books.

CORNELIA
(*Turning away from* GRACE ANNE)
Well, I almost answered her back, but I said to myself, Cornelia, consider the source, she has always been jealous hearted.
(*Turning again to* GRACE ANNE)
How did you like Brother Graham's eulogy for Papa?

GRACE ANNE
All right, I guess, but why did he have to bring up that he was from the North and a Union soldier?

CORNELIA
Because that's what he was.

(*Again turning away from* GRACE ANNE)

Although I wished in my heart he hadn't made so much of it either. And Mrs. Cotman came in looking for me then and began to cry when she saw us together and she said, Oh, thank God the rift in your family has been healed and you two have forgiven each other.

(GRACE ANNE *gives* CORNELIA *a look and goes back to her chair.*)

It was Brother who warned me we'd be having trouble with Grace Anne. We knew the day she eloped to marry Jackson Le Grand, whose family had nothing and who had only just piddly jobs around town like working as a bookkeeper at the cotton gin, that she'd be poor as anything. Anyway, Brother said, Don't tell Mama or Sissie but Grace Anne and Jackson Le Grand are inquiring about how many acres we have. Why? I said. Because I'll bet you every dollar I have she is going to ask to divide it up and give her her share now. Mama will never do it, I said. Never in this world. I know she won't. What are you all whispering about? Mama said. Let me in on the secret. Sissie started crying then saying she missed Papa so much and before I could even try to console her Mama said, as if we had never been told before, Beth is dead. Been dead for ten years. Mama for the last month had out of the blue been saying that. Beth is dead. Been dead for ten years, and that's when we started worrying about Mama's forgetting. That's one thing though she never forgot, no matter in the years to come how mixed up she was. She announced every now and again. Beth is dead. Beth is dead. Been dead for ten years. And no matter how we tried to tell her and say, Mama, Beth has been dead fifteen years or twenty, she would insist on it being ten. Anyway, it wasn't long before we had to tell Mama and Sissie what Grace Anne and her husband were up to. They'd hired a lawyer and he came to us and demanded to see a copy of Papa's will and was telling all over town a great injustice had been done his client, our sister, and that a lot of the estate had been gotten under very cloudy circumstances during the Reconstruction and he was going to look into that part of it too. Well, we didn't know what to do, hire a lawyer for ourselves or go to Grace Anne and plead with her to call off her trifling husband and reason with her that she was to share in the profits from the estate, and finally I made Sissie go see her and she didn't stay long but came back and said Grace Anne wanted nothing except what she had been told by her lawyer was rightfully hers. And what's that? I asked, and Sissie said, A fourth of the land and a fourth of all the assets including our house. Well, she's some kind of fool, I said, if she thinks I will ever let her have that. I'll burn the house down first, I'll— Then Brother said, Calm down, Sister, that's just that lawyer getting her to talk that way, I would try to settle it. How? I said. Make them an offer, he said. Like what? I said. I would offer them ten thousand in cash and five hundred acres of land. Do you think they would settle for that? All I know, he said, is Jackson Le Grand is out of work and they owe everybody in town including the grocery store. Well, try it, I said, and see what happens. I can't go to Grace Anne, he said. We're not speaking. Are you speaking to Jackson? I said. I guess, he said, at least we were yesterday morning. I passed him uptown and he said good morning and I said good morning. Well, go talk to him, I said, and he did and came back and said, He'll settle for fifteen thousand in cash and a thousand acres of land. My God, I said, he's greedy. Didn't I warn you? Brother said. Well, go back and tell him we'll give him twelve thousand dollars and seven hundred fifty acres of land. And by five o'clock that afternoon it was a done deal. We had our lawyer draw up the papers and Mama sign them and we had Jackson off our backs. And they lived pretty high there for awhile, but Jackson was no farmer and the next thing we heard he was borrowing money from the bank. It took him ten years but he finally lost all the land to the bank, but they did get a house out of it. Bought one for three thousand dollars out of the money we gave them. When we heard the bank had taken over the land we had given them I was upset and said, I want to buy our land back, and I did, so we owned once again all the land Papa had left. Jackson is dead now and Grace Anne and her girls live on in the house they bought. She gets by somehow. She gave up all rights and income from the estate when we gave Jackson the land and the money, and she's never asked us for anything since Jackson died. We send the girls money to buy dresses for special occasions like high school graduation and every change of season we tell them to go to a store in town where we have a charge account and get clothes. And we send Grace Anne money as a present on her birthdays. At first she sent it back, but we just kept sending it anyway and lately she's been keeping it. She comes over every now and again now and visits with us. Last Easter she and the girls came over for dinner. The girls are sweet and friendly and come over quite often. Now that Sissie has her baby girl, they seem just crazy about their cousin. Grace Anne sent Sissie a baby gift too when her little girl was born.

The lights fade on CORNELIA's *area and are brought up on* SISSIE's *area.*

SISSIE

I was sitting on the gallery with Mama when Leon Davis, who had been married to my cousin Lenora and had shot and killed her father he said in self defense and had been acquitted, appeared one day. He said he was just riding through Harrison as he had been to Victoria on business and saw us sitting on the porch and decided to stop by and say hello. Cornelia and Brother had gone out to look at the farms that morning. I told him that and he said he was sorry he missed them, and the cook came to the door then and said dinner was ready and Mama asked him if he would have dinner with us and he said no, he didn't want to put us out any, and Mama said, You're not putting anybody out and I insist you eat with us, and he said, Well, if you insist, and we went in the dining room. We had a roast, as I remember, rice and gravy, fresh black eye peas, okra, and molded salad, and I never saw anybody eat the way he did. Talking all the while too. He said did we know he had been given custody of the three children and Lenora had been declared by the courts an unfit mother and had we heard that? We said no, we hadn't, and Brother and Cornelia came in from the country then and joined us at the table and Mama said, Mr. Davis, did you know my oldest girl Beth is dead? Been dead ten years, and he said, I am indeed aware of that sad event and of your husband's death too, and please don't call me Mr. Davis, call me Leon. He'd had three helpings of everything by then and he was telling us about the insurance company he was starting in Houston and that he had been in Victoria talking to potential investors. He stayed for another hour and then said goodbye. Leon Davis began stopping by every two or three days after that. Always, he said, on his way to or from Victoria. He told us one afternoon what happened when he killed our uncle. He explained why he had been acquitted. He said the butcher knife our uncle tried to stab him with was lethal and then he showed us a picture of his three children and I must say they were very sweet looking and he seemed devoted to them. Then Mama said, Sissie, sing the song you were singing when your papa died, and I said, Mama, I can't ever sing that song again, it's too upsetting to me. Then Mama proceeded to tell Mr. Davis all about my singing when Papa died and how I began to scream and they all came running in including the cook and we were all screaming then, and Mama said, Sissie, please sing that song just one more time for Mr. Davis and he said, Leon, remember, and she said, I'm sorry, Leon. Please, Sissie, sing "O, the Clanging Bells of Time" just once more so Leon can hear it. I know by now you might as well let Mama have her way or she'll drive you crazy trying to get it. So I gave in.

(SISSIE *now sings live.*)

"O, the clanging bells of time, Night and day they never cease; We are wearied with their chime, For they do not bring us peace; And we hush our breath to hear, And we strain our eyes to see; If the shores are drawing near, Eternity! Eternity!" It was about that time that Brother came in with Mrs. Carpenter and when Mama saw her she began to holler, Get that hussy out of here, and carried on so poor Mrs. Carpenter and Brother had to leave, and after we quieted Mama down, she turned to Mr. Davis and said, Did you hear about my daughter Beth? She passed away ten years ago today. Mama, I said, she didn't pass away ten years ago and it wasn't on this day. Mama looked at me like I was crazy and Cornelia said,

CORNELIA

Mr. Davis.

SISSIE

(*Imitating Leon*)
Please, please, call me Leon.

CORNELIA

I'm sorry Leon. How is your insurance business coming along?

SISSIE

Splendid, he said. And off he went talking so fast I couldn't
hardly understand a thing he said, but to tell you the truth if
he had been talking slow I couldn't have understood any of it,
for I have no head at all for figures, just none, and I looked
over at Cornelia and she was listening to everything he said
and nodding her head like she approved of his every word and
every figure and I thought to myself, Cornelia is smitten with
him, and then Mama turned to me and said, Would you sing
the song you were singing when your papa died for Mr. Davis?
Leon, remember, Leon, he said. I'm sorry, Mama said, what
was the name of that song, Sissie? "O, the Clanging Bells of
Time," I said. That's right. Sing it for Mr. Davis. Leon, he said.
I'm sorry, Mama said, Leon. I just sang it for him, Mama. You
heard me. Well, sing it again. It comforts me. Wouldn't you
like to hear it again, Mr. Davis? Leon, Leon, he said. Sorry,
Mr. Leon, Mama said. Not Mr. Leon, just Leon, he said. Sing
it honey, Mama said. One more time. Go ahead and sing it,
Sissie, Cornelia said, she'll give us no peace until you do. And
so I sang it.
  (*Again in the distance we hear "O, the Clanging
  Bells of Time." * SISSIE *listens as if remembering the
  singing. The song is prerecorded.*)
Mama began to sing along with me. Then Leon joined in on
the eternities.
  (*And she listens as if remembering hearing her
  mother and Leon join her in singing. This is all
  prerecorded.*)
And Brother came in then and he said, Jackson Le Grand is

dead, he was sitting on a stool at the drugstore and he just
keeled over. Which drugstore? Mama asked, and Brother said
he forgot to ask, and she said to me, Sissie, call Grace Anne
and ask her which drugstore it was, and I said, I'm not going
to do that, Mama, and Brother said, I think somebody should
call over and see how Grace Anne is. I'll call, Cornelia said,
and she did and she came back and said, She's holding up
pretty well, both her girls have been notified in Houston and
are taking the next train home. Maybe I should take the car
and meet them, Brother said. I think that would be nice, I
said. And maybe we should offer to pay for the funeral. I don't
think they have a dime left. Jackson Le Grand was no busi-
nessman and certainly no farmer. Then Mama began singing
"O, the Clanging Bells of Time" and Brother went to the station to meet the girls. Do you think Grace Anne will start
speaking to Brother again now? I asked. Why doesn't she
speak to him? Mama wanted to know. Now you know why,
Mama, I said. I do not, she said. If I ever knew I've forgotten.
Grace Anne heard that Brother said that Jackson married her
for her money and Brother said he thought he had and she
said he had to go to people he said it to and say he was mis-
taken and he refused and she said unless he did she would
never speak to him again. Well, she did start speaking to him
again, and I must say Brother was a rock. He made all the funeral arrangements for her, all of which the estate paid for,
and they had Jackson Le Grand on view at their house for two
days before the funeral and Brother insisted on sitting up with
his body both nights so Grace Anne could get some sleep, and
Cornelia and I went downtown and bought suitable dresses
for Grace Anne and the girls to wear at the funeral, and Cornelia offered to have people come back to our house after the
service since the living room of our house was three times the
size of their living room, and Grace Anne thanked her but said
she'd rather see people in her own house and that's what she
did. After the cemetery Mama went back with us to Grace
Anne's house, and I must say the neighbors and friends sent
in delicious food and in the middle of it all Mama turned to
me and said, Sissie, sing "O, the Clanging Bells of Time." I

had been a little hurt, to tell you the truth, that Grace Anne hadn't asked me to sing at Jackson's funeral, but instead asked Pansy Fullmore who always sings off key. Pansy was sitting next to me in Grace Anne's living room and to get Mama off the subject of my singing I said, Pansy, I thought you sang wonderfully today. Oh, thank you, she said, but Mama would-n't give up and she kept after me to sing "O, the Clanging Bells of Time" and I looked over at Cornelia and Grace Anne and they both said to me to please sing it and get it over with and so I did. Mama joining in again.

The lights fade as we hear prerecorded SISSIE *and her mother singing "O, the Clanging Bells of Time." The lights are brought up on* GRACE ANNE'S *area.* GRACE ANNE *is again sewing.*

GRACE ANNE

Brother and I made up, after Jackson died, and it was a relief to me. He came over real often then. He couldn't take Mrs. Carpenter over to Mama's house because of the way Mama carried on when she saw them together and so Brother started bringing her over here and we had nice visits together. Brother was all excited that he might get a job with Leon Davis when he started his insurance company. He said if he had any money of his own he would invest in it, because it was going to make somebody rich. He said he was trying to get Cornelia to invest for the estate, and she wanted to, but Leon wouldn't accept her money because he said he wouldn't sleep nights feeling so responsible. Why, if anything happened and he lost her money he would never forgive himself. Brother said he thought Leon was sweet on Cornelia and he thought she liked him too. Leon was there almost every day and Mama was crazy about him too and Sissie and Sissie's little girl called him Uncle Leon. Brother came over by himself the other af-ternoon and said he had decided when he got his job with the insurance company he was going to marry Mrs. Carpenter. He didn't care what Mama would say. He said he had already asked Mrs. Carpenter if they married would she sign an agree-ment not to ever sue for part of the estate like my husband and I did, and he said Mrs. Carpenter would gladly agree to that. Then Leon agreed to let Cornelia invest in his company and it was to be done in three payments. Fifteen thousand dollars each. She gave him the first payment on a Friday and Leon on that day told Brother he now had a job and he was going to have an office in Victoria and Houston and which office would he like to be in? And Brother said let me ask Mrs. Carpenter where she would like to live, because we're going to be married, and Leon asked him when and he said, As soon as I can get the license and I'd like you to be my best man and Leon said he'd be honored and where would the ceremony take place, in a church? Brother said no, he was going to ask me if they could be married at my house, which he did, and I said he certainly could. Then he came over and Mama was raising a fit about his marrying and said she wouldn't have Mrs. Carpenter in her house married or not and he asked after the wedding could they stay with me until he found a place for them to live in Houston when he started work for Leon Davis and I said they certainly could and he said he would pay rent for as long as he stayed and I thanked him and I said that would certainly be a help to me, as I had decided next year to get in a little extra income and rent my spare room to a schoolteacher now that my girls were grown and living in Houston. And I asked Brother if Mrs. Carpenter had any family that would be coming for the wedding and he said no, that both her parents were dead and she was an only child. I then asked him if he was going to have anybody in town to the wedding and he said no, he wanted it small and intimate and he would just have his three sisters and Sissie's husband if he could get away from his job in Houston and her daughter, of course, and my two girls if they could get away from their jobs in Houston and our mama if she would come and Leon Davis who was going to be his best man and maybe I could be the matron of honor and I said I thought I best not as I had turned down Sissie when my feelings were still hurt over Papa's treatment of Jackson. Anyway, it turned out that Sissie's husband and my two girls couldn't get away from their jobs in Houston and Mama wouldn't come, but Sissie agreed to sing, "Oh, Promise Me" and Cornelia ordered flowers for the house so the living room looked real pretty and festive. Mrs. Carpenter was a

Baptist and Brother was a Methodist, although neither of them even went to church except at Easter and Christmas, so they decided to ask the Episcopalian minister to marry them and he accepted. We decided to have the wedding at twelve noon and Cornelia said she would bring food to eat after the ceremony and Brother told me for their honeymoon Cornelia said the estate was paying for a weekend at a hotel of their choice in Houston. At ten o'clock Sissie and her girl and Cornelia came with the flowers and the food Cornelia had prepared. Cornelia is the Big Boss now, you know, just like Beth used to be, but I don't say anything. I just let her take over even if it is my house, and while Cornelia was busy arranging flowers Sissie came over to me.

SISSIE

(*Whispering*)
We may be having another wedding soon.

GRACE ANNE

Who is that going to be?

SISSIE

(*Whispering*)
Cornelia and Leon Davis, but don't say a word about it until she tells you.

GRACE ANNE

How do you know about it? Did Cornelia tell you?

SISSIE

No. I heard Leon ask Mama's permission to marry her.

GRACE ANNE

Is he going to sign an agreement like your husband did and Mrs. Carpenter has done? But before she could tell me all of it Mrs. Carpenter came in all dressed up for the wedding and you've heard, I'm sure, that saying all brides are beautiful, but I must say in Mrs. Carpenter's case it was true, as I always thought she was attractive and pleasant enough looking but nothing to write home about but I'll have to say on this day she was just lovely looking. Then Brother came in and Mama.

I almost dropped over dead when I saw Mama, but I didn't act surprised at all. I thought Mrs. Carpenter looked scared to death like she had no idea now what to expect, whether to go on over and speak to Mama or run out of the room. Finally, I saw her take a deep breath and go over to Mama and say hello. Mama looked at her like she had never seen her before in her life and then Brother said, Mama, you remember Mrs. Carpenter, and Mama looked her up and down and said, Is she the one you are marrying? Yes, Mama, Brother said. Well, I wish you both happiness, she said and then she looked around the room and said, Where is Leon? And Brother said, He's on his way, Mama, the wedding isn't until twelve, and then Mama said, Where is Cornelia?

CORNELIA

I'm here, Mama.

GRACE ANNE

Did she tell you her news? Mama said. Leon Davis asked her to marry him.

CORNELIA

Mama.

She starts to the table in the center of the stage and sits.

GRACE ANNE

Nothing makes me happier, Cornelia, Mama said. I'm fond of Leon Davis. Brother said, All we need now is my best man who'll be here in two minutes and we can get started.

GRACE ANNE, *too, sits at the center table as the lights fade. The lights are brought up on* SISSIE's *area.*

SISSIE

Well, he wasn't there in two minutes, nor in five, nor in ten, nor in twenty, nor in thirty. I hope he's all right, I said, I hope he hasn't had an accident. Where is he coming from? the Episcopalian minister asked. Houston, Brother said. What are we waiting for? Mama kept asking every five minutes. Leon, Brother kept telling her. When forty minutes had passed Cornelia said, I'll call his apartment. She went into the next room then and we waited another five minutes and she came back out. No one answered the phone, she said. I guess we'd better get started, Brother said. I'll have to be my own best man. Everybody sat down and I went to the piano and I began to sing "Oh, Promise Me."

> (*Again it's* SISSIE's *memory of singing the song, and we hear it continuing all through her speech. Again the song is prerecorded.*)

And Grace Anne began to cry in the middle of the song and I looked over at Cornelia and she looked like death, I thought, but she wasn't crying and I looked at my daughter and at Mama and Mrs. Carpenter and I heard a car down the street and I said a prayer to myself, Please, God, let it be Leon Davis, but before I could even finish my prayer I heard the car pass Grace Anne's house and head on into town. I finished singing then and the Episcopalian minister nodded to Brother and Mrs. Carpenter and they all went to the front of the room and the preacher or pastor or father or whatever they call the minister of the Episcopalian church was about to begin the service when Cornelia let out a sob and ran out of the room. Where's Cornelia going? Mama asked. Sh, Mama, I said. Don't sh me. I want to know where Cornelia is going. Maybe home, Mama, I don't think she's feeling well. What's wrong with her? Never mind, Mama. She'll be all right. How do you know? Mama, Brother said, may we please go on with the service? I'm worried about Cornelia, Mama said. I'll go see to her, Mama, I said. I want to go with you. All right, come on, and I took her out of the house. Then Grace Anne told me later that the preacher waited a minute until they heard my car start and go down the road and then he went on with the service. It was all very sad, as you can imagine. As far as any of us knew Cornelia never heard a word from Leon Davis, nor did she ever see a penny of that fifteen thousand dollars again. She never discussed any of it with me ever, nor did I expect her to, and Grace Anne said she never mentioned it to her either, nor did she to Brother until one day she called him into her office at the house and showed him a clipping from a San Diego, California, paper. It was an account of Leon Davis's death. Who sent that to you? Brother asked. She handed him the envelope and he saw there was no name and no return address on it, and there was nothing inside the envelope but the newspaper clipping. The Second World War came along about then and the town was often filled with soldiers and German prisoners of war were brought in and kept at the fairgrounds and we used to get in our car and ride out and look at them now and again. Farm prices went sky high and the farmers began to prosper again and Brother and Mrs. Carpenter were able to buy a nice little house of their own. The street around our house began changing, getting more and more commercial. Filling stations and fast food restaurants and used car lots until finally our house was the only one left. Cornelia had a chance to sell it for commercial property but she refused. Brother always said that cotton farming began to change after the war and the cotton picking machines and tractors began to replace the wagons and mules and tenant farmers and their families. Brother said it seemed to him there was nothing for Cornelia to do but change with the times and she finally agreed. She decided she had to then go out and tell the tenants and their wives and their children that they had to leave. Anyway, it was all very depressing but I didn't let it get me down. Whenever I got worried or depressed, I would just sing to myself "Brighten the Corner."

SISSIE *sings as she goes to her chair and the lights fade. The lights are brought up on* GRACE ANNE'S *area.*

GRACE ANNE

Sissie died. She went to sleep one night and never woke up. Sissie's daughter went to live with her father in Houston and Cornelia was alone in that big old house with just Mama. Once in a while Cornelia would bring Mama over to see me and Mama was talking all the time now about Beth and Papa and Sissie like they were still alive. She had Papa now a general in the Union Army and that he had been invited by the town of Harrison to come in after the Civil War to bring order to the town and to the county. She had it now they had given him several medals for his service to the town and the county. When I asked her where the medals were she said she had

given them to Leon Davis to keep for her and he'd be bringing them back one day. Cornelia just shook her head and
sighed at that. She goes on like this sometimes day and night,
she said. She is wearing me out. I think I'm going to have to
hire a colored woman to come in and stay with her. I don't
blame you at all, I told her. A week later Brother told me Cornelia had hired two colored women to stay with Mama. One
in the daytime and one at night. That fall during cotton season I rode out to the farms to see the cotton picking machines
at work. I had never seen one before. It was quite a sight, and
can you believe it, in all these years I had never seen any of
Papa's farms before? It's beautiful land. It was as fine as any
land in the county, Brother said.

*She begins her sewing again as the lights fade. The lights are brought
up on* CORNELIA's *area. In the distance we hear cars and an occasional
truck pass.*

CORNELIA

I have two very refined and lovely colored ladies staying with
Mama. One of them is Rosa Gilbert who is very religious and
reads the Book of Psalms all the time. She has begun reading
them aloud to Mama and it seems to calm her. She doesn't talk
constantly about the past the way she used to. She told Rosa
Gilbert one day about Papa being a general in the Union
Army and then she told her he had personally sent for some
Quakers to come here to teach the children of the slaves after
the war to read and write and because of that the Ku Klux
Klan threatened to burn our house down and if it hadn't been
for his friend Colonel Hawkins it might have happened. But
Colonel Hawkins stood guard over our house with his gun one
night and frightened the Ku Klux Klan away. I told Rosa of
course that it might be true, but I doubt it as I'd never heard
Papa speak of it.
       (*She pulls a box from under her chair and opens it.*)
Anyway, I decided then to go up to the attic where Sissie used
to play paper dolls with her friends when it rained and look in
a trunk that had some of Papa's things stored away. I found

Papa's discharge papers from the Union Army. He was a private and I found some old canceled checks and bills of sale for the land he had bought all those years ago and found his army uniform.

(*She takes the uniform from the box.*)

I showed it to Mama and said, Mama, see Papa was only a private, but she spit at me and ordered me out of the room.

(*She puts the uniform aside and gets out of the chair.*)

I wonder how much longer I can go on. Farming is getting so expensive now. I don't know what I'm going to do. I promised Papa I would never sell off the land, and I never have except for that time with Grace Anne and Jackson Le Grand and fortunately I was able to buy that back. And I certainly don't want to sell now, although who am I holding on to it for? Sissie is dead. Grace Anne? How much longer will she be here? She's five years older than I am. Brother? He's seven years older. Mama? Sissie's daughter or Grace Anne's girls? Sissie said her daughter told her if the land was hers she would sell it in a minute and I expect she would.

(*A pause*)

It almost killed me the day I had to go out and tell the tenants I had to change how I was farming or I'd lose everything. I don't know whether they believed me or not. Old Jake Tillman and his wife had been on their place nearly forty years and his daddy ten years before him, anyway they cried and I cried when I told them the fix I was in. Some of the others just didn't look at me while I was talking to them. Just stared down at their feet and I couldn't even see their faces. They all said they understood, but I'm not sure they did. I gave each of them a little money and six months grace to relocate.

(*A pause*)

I got a letter with no address or name on the envelope with just a clipping inside saying Leon Davis had died. I'll go to my grave wondering who sent me that clipping. I didn't tell anybody not even Brother, but a year after Leon Davis disappeared I called my cousin Lenora who was his wife and I asked her if she knew where he was and she asked me, Why,

does he owe you money? If he does, she said, you'll never get
it. He owes everybody in the city of Houston. He got a lot of
fools to invest in some scheme he had about an insurance
company and once he got their money he just disappeared.
What about the children? What about the children? she said.
Didn't he have custody of them? Who told you that lie? He's
never gone near his children since he killed Papa all those
years ago. Never sent them a dime either.

(*A pause. She points to the plaque behind her.*)
Did you see the plaque the Historical Society is putting up on
our house? We're the oldest house in town now. There used
to be ten or fifteen older, some right on this street, but they
were all sold off long ago, and replaced by filling stations and
God knows what all. Oh, well.

(*She goes to the table and picks up a document.*)
The plaque reads: The Joseph Thompson house, built in 1870
by Joseph Thompson, a soldier in the Union Army, has been
listed in the National Register of Historic Places by the
United States Department of the Interior. I showed it to
Mama and she said they have it wrong. He wasn't in the
Union Army, he was in the Confederate Army and he was
general and he was wounded at the Battle of Shiloh. I
thought, Well, tomorrow she'll go back to his being a general
in the Union Army, but at breakfast the first thing she said to
me was, Are you gonna have that lie changed about his being
in the Union Army? There are a group of people coming over
here to celebrate the placing of the plaque on our house and
they asked me if I would have Mama here to say a few words
to them about Papa and the history of the house, and I said
that would not be possible and they would have to settle for
me or my brother or Grace Anne, for I knew if Mama got out
here she would go on about his being a general in the Union
Army or the Confederate Army and the Ku Klux Klan and
God knows what all. Brother and his wife and Grace Anne
will come over and I've made some coffee and will serve that
and fruitcake to the guests after the ceremony. One lady told
me at the supermarket she wouldn't have a plaque like that
on her house as perfect strangers will see it as they drive by

and will stop and knock on your door day and night asking all kinds of questions.

(*Traffic noises are heard.*)

Hear that traffic? It gets worse all the time. It used to be so quiet here. When Beth was sick and we brought her home to die the men in the town covered the street with straw so there'd be no noise when the wagons and the horses went by. I wonder what they would have to do now to stop the noise. I wonder sometimes about Beth. Did we do the right thing in telling her she was going to be all right?

(*In the distance we hear* MRS. THOMPSON *calling,*
"Cornelia. Cornelia. Cornelia.")

That's Mama calling me. I know what she wants. Mama is going to ask me to get Sissie to sing "O, the Clanging Bells of Time" and there is no sense in telling her Sissie is dead because she won't believe me, and the only way to shut her up is to go in the next room and pretend I'm Sissie and sing it for her, pitiful voice that I have.

(*She goes to her chair and picks up the uniform
and slowly starts across the stage singing "O, the
Clanging Bells of Time."*)

"O, the clanging bells of time, Night and day they never cease; We are wearied with their chime, For they do not bring us peace; And we hush our breath to hear, And we strain our eyes to see; If the shores are drawing near,

(*And* GRACE ANNE *and* SISSIE *join her in Eternity.*)

Eternity! Eternity!"

As the lights go down and the stage is in darkness.

The Actor

The world premiere of *The Actor* was presented at the Royal National Theatre in London on July 12, 2002, directed by Colin Snell.

Cast

HORACE JUNIOR	*Ben Hynes*
ELIZABETH	*Laura Derkins*
JIM	*Ben Smith*
HORACE SENIOR	*Michael Stacey*
MISS PRATHER	*Olivia Brown*

EARLY SPRING—1932

A section of a hall in the Harrison high school. HORACE ROBEDAUX JR.,
*fifteen, is there. He looks at his wrist watch, he hums to himself several
bars of "Brother, Can You Spare a Dime," looks up and down the hallway,
and then begins to sing to himself snatches of "Brother, Can You Spare a
Dime."*

HORACE

(*Singing*)
"Once I built a railroad,
Made it run,
Made it race against time.
Once I built a railroad,
Now it's done,
Brother, can you spare a dime?"

Two boys, a year or so older than HORACE, *come down the hall each with
a girl. They are* ARCHIE *and* VARD. SUSAN KATE *is with* ARCHIE *and*
LOUISE *is with* VARD. *They carry school books.*

SUSAN KATE & LOUISE

Hello, Horace.

HORACE

Hi.

ARCHIE

Hi, Horace.

HORACE

Hi.

VARD

Rudolph Valentino, what's new?

HORACE

Not much.

> (*They walk down the hall.* HORACE *talks to the au-
> dience as to a close friend.*)

I hate it when somebody calls me Rudolph Valentino. I was
walking in front of Rugeley's Drugstore yesterday on the way
to the post office when old Blowhard Mayor Douglas came
out of the drugstore and called out in a loud voice, "Hey there,
Valentino," and all the old men sitting in front of the drugstore
laughed like it was the funniest thing they had ever heard. I
didn't think it was funny at all, but I pretended like I did and
I just said, "Pretty well, thank you; Mr. Mayor," and walked on.
When I went to the store to watch it so my daddy could go for
his afternoon coffee, I told him about the mayor calling out,
"Hello, Rudolph Valentino," as I went by, and he said I
shouldn't be sensitive, that he was just being friendly. Maybe
so, but I'm not so sure and I still don't like it.

Another boy, CECIL, *walks by.*

CECIL

Hello, Rudolph Valentino.

HORACE

Heh.

> (*The boy continues on.*)

This Rudolph Valentino business all started, you know, when
I won the prize for the best actor at the State Drama Festival.
They gave me a medal for being the best actor, but my
teacher, Miss Prather, accepted it for the school, and it's been
two weeks since the festival and she still hasn't given my
medal to me. Miss Prather asked me to meet her after school.
She says she has something for me. Maybe it's my medal.
Anyway, if that's not what she wants I decided today to ask her
for it. I hate doing it, but my mother says she is a busy teacher

and has just forgotten she has it, and she won't mind at all my reminding her she has it. I hope she won't. Anyway, I'm going to do it. I want the medal, so I can keep it in my room, and it will be there to remind me of what it was like when I got the medal. Miss Prather said it was very exciting when the three judges called out her name and asked to speak with her, and she said she couldn't imagine what they wanted, and when she got to them they said, "Is that Robedaux boy playing the drug addict afflicted or is he acting?" and she said, "It's acting." "Very well," they said, "he gets first prize as best actor," and she said she waited around a few minutes longer hoping they were going to say our one act play won the prize for the best play, but when they handed her my medal and said, "Thank you, you may return to your seat now," she knew we hadn't won best play or best production, only best actor.

SUSAN KATE *comes back in.*

SUSAN KATE

Hello, Horace.

HORACE

Hello.

SUSAN KATE

Waiting for Miss Prather?

HORACE

Uh. Huh.

SUSAN KATE

I just saw her in the auditorium.

HORACE

Thanks.

(SUSAN KATE *goes on.*)

The next day at school in our speech class she told everybody about my winning best actor, and it was all over school by then anyway, and she said in her opinion no one could help being moved at the moment I confessed to my roommates that I was an addict and needed drugs, and then she asked me to wait after class and I did, thinking she would give me my

medal, but she never mentioned the medal but wanted to
know if I was interested in being in the senior play which
would start rehearsing in a few weeks. I said I would be, and
I wanted to tell her I wanted to be an actor, but I didn't know
how to. I don't know why I couldn't tell her. Of all the people
I know around here she'd likely be the one to understand and
encourage me, but I don't know. I just can't bring myself to
say out loud, I want to be an actor, not a lawyer or a doctor,
an actor.

CECIL *walks by.*

                              CECIL
You're still here, Rudolph Valentino?

                              HORACE
What does it look like?
        (CECIL *goes on.*)
I've known for a long time too that's what I wanted to be.
Since I was thirteen. You see I used to go for walks in the
evening with my mother and daddy and we'd always pass on
our walks Mr. Armstrong's house. I could always tell when we
were approaching his house no matter how dark a night it was,
because the fences around his house were covered with honeysuckle vines and you could smell the honeysuckle a block
away. Anyway, Mr. Armstrong, a very old man, would always
be sitting in the dark on his gallery and as we passed my daddy
would always call out, "Good evening, Mr. Armstrong," and he
would always answer, "Just fine, thank you. How are you?"
even though my daddy had never asked how he was but only
wished him a good evening, and my daddy explained to me
that he always answered that way because he was deaf and
couldn't hear what my daddy said and only imagined what he
said, and then he would always add, "You know Mr. Armstrong
was working in the cotton fields in Mississippi when he got a
call to come to Texas to preach. And that's what he did. He
came here to preach." I had never heard of anyone getting a
call before to preach or anything else, so I asked my parents
a lot of questions about getting a call. Could anyone get a call?
They weren't sure about that since Mr. Armstrong was the

only person they ever knew who actually had gotten a call. "Is
that because he is a Baptist, is that why he got a call?" I asked.
My mother said no, she had heard about Methodists and Epis-
copalians getting a call to preach although she hadn't met anyone personally that had except Mr. Armstrong.

LOUISE *and* SUSAN KATE *approach. They are giggling.*

> LOUISE
>
> I'm glad you're still here, Horace.

> SUSAN KATE
>
> Horace—
> (*They again begin to giggle.*)
> You ask him.

> LOUISE
>
> No, you ask him. You said you would ask him.

> SUSAN KATE
>
> All right. Horace.

> HORACE
>
> Yes.

> SUSAN KATE
>
> Are you going to the dance on Friday night?

> HORACE
>
> Yes.

> SUSAN KATE
>
> Do you have a date?

> HORACE
>
> Not yet.

> SUSAN KATE
>
> Would you do us a favor?

> HORACE
>
> What?

> SUSAN KATE
>
> Marie Jackson doesn't have a date and would you please,
> please be nice and ask her to go?

LOUISE

Please, please.

HORACE

Did she ask you to ask me?

SUSAN KATE

No. Did she Louise?

LOUISE

No.

HORACE

I thought she was going steady with Cecil.

SUSAN KATE

He dropped her.

LOUISE

Susan Kate you shouldn't say that. She would be so upset if she knew you said that.

SUSAN KATE

Well, he did.

LOUISE

I know but you shouldn't be spreading it all over school.

SUSAN KATE

Will you ask her, Horace? She's very upset.

LOUISE

We found her crying in the girls' room.

HORACE

I asked her for a date once and she turned me down.

SUSAN KATE

Please, Horace.

LOUISE

Please, please, Horace.

HORACE

Well, you go ask her if she wants me to ask her and then I'll see.

SUSAN KATE

Thanks. We'll be right back.

They leave.

HORACE

Anyway, a year later when I turned thirteen I got a call, just as sure as Mr. Armstrong did. Not to preach but to be an actor. I kept that to myself for a month and then I told Todd Lewis, who was my best friend before he had to move away, about it and he said if I wanted his advice I'd keep it to myself as people would think I was peculiar wanting to be something like that. And for good or bad I've never told anyone else. I asked my mother one time what she thought Mr. Armstrong did when he got his call and she said she couldn't be sure, but she imagined he fell on his knees in the cotton fields and prayed about it and listened to what God wanted him to do and God worked things out for him so he could come to Texas and preach, and that's what I did. I prayed about it and asked God what I should do and the very next year Miss Prather came here to teach fresh out of college, and she put on plays, and that was encouraging to me and I found out from my daddy where Mr. Dude Arthur's tent show would be in the next few weeks. He always had his itinerary because Mr. Arthur was a customer and often wrote my daddy to send him clothes while he was on the road with his tent show. He asked me why I wanted his address. I said just to write and tell him how much I liked his tent show and he said that was a good idea as Mr. Arthur and his brother Mickey were always very good customers, even though Mr. Arthur was often short of cash and had to have extended credit, since the tent show business was having hard times because of the movies. Anyway, I learned he was going to be in Tyler, Texas, in two weeks and I wrote him there, care of general delivery, which is what my father said I should do, and I reminded him in the letter who I was and that I sometimes waited on him in my father's store when he came to Harrison, and I would appreciate it if he wouldn't mention to anyone, not even my daddy, but the next time he was in Harrison, I would like very much to see him as I wanted to ask him how you go about being an actor. He never answered my letter, so I figured he had never gotten it. So last summer when he came here with his tent show, I went over to the boardinghouse where he stayed with his wife and brother Mickey, who plays all the juvenile parts in the tent show, and I told Mr. Arthur I had written him a letter, and had he gotten it. He was drunk and said he didn't remember any letter, what was it about. And I said I wanted advice as I wanted to be an actor. He said why in the name of God, and I said because I wanted to, and I believed I had a call to be one and he said, well, you're a fool if you think that and get over it. Mrs. Arthur came in then and said, "Dude, sober up! You have a show tonight," and I left.

SUSAN KATE *and* LOUISE *come back in.*

SUSAN KATE

She has a date.

HORACE

Who with?

LOUISE

Cecil.

HORACE

I thought he'd dumped her.

LOUISE

We thought so too, but I guess he changed his mind.

SUSAN KATE

Thank you, anyway. I told her you wanted to ask her for a date, but you were too shy.

HORACE

I didn't say I wanted to ask her for a date.

SUSAN KATE

Don't bite my head off. I thought you wanted to ask her for a date.

HORACE

I certainly did not say that. I said to ask her if she wanted me to ask her for a date and then I'd see.

LOUISE

Come on, Sarah Kate. Let's don't stand here and argue. I have
to get home or my mama will kill me.

They leave.

HORACE

The next day Dude Arthur came to my daddy's store and in
front of me told my daddy that I had come to see him at his
boardinghouse and that I had written him a letter about wanting to be an actor, and after he left, my daddy asked was I out
of my mind. Being an actor and in a tent show was a terrible
way to make a living, and Dude Arthur had told him he was
giving up after this season because he was broke, and I said,
"I guess I shouldn't have, but I did." I said, "Well, Daddy,
that's no worse than being a cotton farmer or a merchant, they
are always broke too." "But at least, young man"—he always
calls me young man when he's mad at me—"at least, young
man, I have a roof over my head and I manage to always put
food on the table, and I'm not drunk half the time, wandering
around the country with only a mortgaged tent to my name."
Daddy said he hoped now that this would be the end of such
foolishness, and I decided then and there, call or not, I would
give it up. But when my mother read in the Houston papers
that the Ben Greet Players would be in Houston for a week
with their Shakespearean repertoire, she said she thought it
would be nice for me to go and see them in one of their plays.
She wrote my grandmother, my daddy's mother, who lives in
Houston and goes to see plays all the time, and she wrote back
to send me on to Houston and she would go with me to the
play. I went to Houston but she had a headache and couldn't
go to the play with me after all. She lived on the streetcar line
and she said if I went by myself she would give me real clear
directions so I couldn't possibly get lost. So she wrote out for
me how to get to the theater and back by the streetcar, and I
took the streetcar and I got to the theater just fine, but when
I got off the streetcar I saw across the street a sign in front of
another theater that read Florence Reed in The Shanghai
Gesture. I heard my Houston grandmother say that was a
wicked play and one that shouldn't be allowed in Houston,

and so I don't know what devil got inside me suggesting I go see The Shanghai Gesture instead of the Ben Greet Players, but whatever it was, I took my money my mother had given me for the Ben Greet Players and I bought a ticket to see Florence Reed, and I guess it was wicked and immoral like my grandmother in Houston said, but I thought it was wonderful and I said to myself I have to be an actor now somehow, someway.

MARIE JACKSON *and* CECIL *come in.*

MARIE

Oh, Horace. I'm so touched you wanted to ask me to the dance.

HORACE

Well—

MARIE

Don't be shy. I would love to go with you. But Cecil had just asked me when the girls came to tell me you were too shy to ask me.

CECIL

Are you shy, Valentino?

HORACE

No, I'm not shy.

MARIE

Why do you call him Valentino?

CECIL

Because he won an acting prize. Isn't that right Valentino?

HORACE

Yes.

MARIE

You did? Oh that's so sweet.

CECIL

Didn't you know that? Miss Prather announced it in study hall.

MARIE

When? What day?

CECIL

What day? I forget. What day was it, Horace?

HORACE

I forget too.

MARIE

It must have been the day I was home sick. What kind of part did you play, Horace?

CECIL

He played a dope fiend.

MARIE

How do you know? Did you see it?

CECIL

No. I heard about it.

MARIE

I wish I could have seen it.

They leave.

HORACE

Anyway, I never told my mother or my Houston grand-mother I didn't see the Ben Greet Players and when they asked me what play of Shakespeare I had seen I said Julius Caesar because I had read that play in English class my junior year and I had memorized the "Friends, Romans, countrymen, lend me your ears" speech for the class, and I knew if they asked me questions about the play I could answer them. I didn't realize Adelaide Martin, one of my mother's friends, had gone into Houston that same day to see the Ben Greet Players and when she got back she called my mother to tell her about it and my mother said I had been there too and had liked it a lot, and Adelaide said she didn't care for it as she thought the Romeo and Juliet looked middle aged and were too old for their parts. "Romeo and Juliet," Mama said. "That's not what Horace saw," she said. "He saw Julius Caesar." "Julius Caesar? Did he go to the matinee or the evening show?" Mother said to the matinee and Adelaide said that's the one she attended and there was no Julius Caesar, but Romeo and Juliet. When I got home from school my mother confronted me with this and I had to admit what I had done. She asked me what The Shanghai Gesture was about and I said it took place in a Shanghai brothel and that's all she had to know. She said I was deceitful and should be ashamed of myself going to a play like that. I guess I should have been, but I wasn't. All I could think about was how Florence Reed reacted when, as the madame of the brothel, she heard that her daughter, who she hadn't seen in years, turned up as one of the girls in the brothel.

(*A pause. He sings again.*)
"Once I built a railroad,
Made it run,
Made it run against time.
Once I built a railroad,
Now it's done,
Brother, can you spare a dime?"

I love to hear Russ Colombo sing that song. My father hates the song. He says it's too depressing. He says he likes positive songs like "Happy Days Are Here Again." He says the country needs to have songs like that so they'll be in an optimistic mood and not depressed all the time.

ARCHIE *and* VARD *come back by.*

ARCHIE

Are you still here?

HORACE

What does it look like?

VARD

What are you hanging around here for?

HORACE

I'm waiting for Miss Prather.

ARCHIE

You have a crush on Miss Prather, don't you?

HORACE

No, I don't have a crush on Miss Prather.

VARD

What are you always hanging around her for?

HORACE

I'm not always hanging around her. I have to see her about something.

VARD

About what?

HORACE

None of your business.

VARD

You're in a good mood today.

They start out.

ARCHIE

(*Calling back*)
Have you decided what college you're going to apply to?

HORACE

Not yet.

VARD

I'm applying to A&M.

They continue on.

HORACE

Everybody's applying for college that can afford to go. Next time someone asks me about college I think I'll just come right out and say I'm not going to college. Not ever. I'm going to be an actor. Yeah. I bet you will. I can't even tell my mother and father. I'm almost scared to, because how my daddy blew up at the store when Dude Arthur told him I wanted to be an actor. I tried last night to tell them. We were sitting together on the porch and there was no moon and it was pitch dark. I could see lightning bugs everywhere and I thought, I'll tell them now because it's dark and I don't have to look at their faces when I tell them, but dark or not

I couldn't get the words out. My daddy was going on about the Depression and how hard a time he was having and how bad he felt that he couldn't send me to college this year, and I was saying to myself the whole time, I don't want to go to college, so don't worry about it, but dark or not I just couldn't get the words out. Mama said, "Are you feeling alright, Son? You seem so quiet." "Yes, ma'am," I said, "I feel fine." And my daddy started on about college again and he kept saying over and over he's going to work extra hard at the store in the fall when the crops come in, and he knows Roosevelt is going to work a miracle and lick the Depression and we'll all have money again like in 1918 and he'll be able to send me to college next fall. "Yes, sir," I said. "I appreciate your concern." Then he said, "Well, I'm going to bed. I have to work tomorrow. You better get to bed too, Son. You have school tomorrow." "Yes, sir," I said, and Mama said, "Kiss me goodnight, Son," and I did and went to my room. My daddy and my mother stayed on the porch awhile longer. I undressed and got into bed, but I could hear them talking on the porch and my mother said, "He's so young, hon. If I had to do it over again, I swear I would never have started him in school at five years old. Fifteen is so young to be graduating from high school." "He's not a child, hon," my father said. "He's a young man. He'll be sixteen by the time he graduates."

DOROTHY PRATHER, *twenty-one, comes in. She has some books and papers and a briefcase.*

DOROTHY

Forgive me, Horace, for being late. I got detained by an irate mother, who thinks her precious child should have gotten an A instead of a B. What did you want to see me about?

HORACE

That's alright.

DOROTHY

I wanted to give you a copy of the play I'm doing with you seniors. I want you to read it and tell me how you like it.

HORACE

Thank you.

She hands him the play.

DOROTHY

It's called *Not So Long Ago*. It was done in New York several years ago. Eva Le Gallienne played the lead. She is a very gifted actress. She played in Lilliom in New York, you know.

HORACE

Did she?

DOROTHY

Yes. Anyway, that's all I wanted.

HORACE

Yes, ma'am.
   (*She starts away.*)
Miss Prather. I keep meaning to ask you. I never saw the medal I was given for best actor. Do you have it?

She laughs.

DOROTHY

Oh, Horace, I feel terrible. I didn't tell you because I kept hoping it would turn up. I lost your medal.

HORACE

Yes, ma'am.

DOROTHY

I left it at the San Antonio high school after talking to the judges.

HORACE

I see.

DOROTHY

It wasn't until I got back here that I realized what I'd done. I called right away and asked if someone had found it, and they said no, but they'd look out for it and if they found it they would get it to me. Obviously they haven't.

HORACE

Uh. Huh.

DOROTHY

You see, when the judges called me up to speak to them about your acting I thought they were calling me to say our play had won first place in the contest and when I realized we hadn't, I was so disappointed I just forgot about your medal. I think I left it on the judges' table or somewhere in the auditorium. Anyway, you won and that's what counts. I'm sorry I lost your medal.

HORACE

That's alright. Miss Prather—

DOROTHY

(*Interrupting*)

And Horace, I've been meaning to ask you, did you ever know any addicts?

HORACE

No, not really. I used to see Miss Sadie Underwood walking past my daddy's store whenever I clerked there on Saturday's and after school. And I heard someone tell my daddy as she walked by that she was addicted to paregoric. My daddy says you can get addicted to Coca-Colas. He says Strachen New-some was addicted to Coca-Colas, drank nine or ten a day until they ate the lining of his stomach and he died from drinking too many Coca-Colas.

DOROTHY

My heavens. Well. Nice to see you, Horace. Read the play and tell me what you think.

HORACE

Yes, ma'am.

(*She starts away.*)

Miss Prather?

DOROTHY

Yes.

HORACE

I haven't told my mother and daddy about this yet, so please
don't say anything about it to anyone.
    (*A pause*)
My daddy can't afford to send me to college next year.

DOROTHY

I'm sorry, Horace.

HORACE

That's alright, but he says he hopes to be able to send me the
following year.

DOROTHY

A year will go quickly, you know.

HORACE

Yes, ma'am, but I don't want to go to college.

DOROTHY

Never?

HORACE

Never.

DOROTHY

Oh, Horace.

HORACE

Never.

DOROTHY

Why, Horace?

HORACE

Well—
    (*A pause. Then almost blurting out.*)
I want to be an actor.

DOROTHY

Oh, well.

HORACE

I've heard there are acting schools.

DOROTHY

Yes, there are.

HORACE

Do you know about acting schools?

DOROTHY

A little. How do your parents feel about this?

HORACE

I don't know. I haven't told them.

DOROTHY

I think you should tell them, Horace.

HORACE

I'm going to. I read in the Chronicle the other day that someone from Houston was studying acting in Pasadena, California.

DOROTHY

Yes, there is a school there. At the Pasadena Playhouse. They have summer courses, and as a matter of fact I was thinking of taking some courses myself and I thought it might be interesting to go to an acting school that had a summer course. Pasadena was one and I was considering the American Academy as the other.

HORACE

Where is that?

DOROTHY

In New York City.

HORACE

Oh. Are they expensive, Miss Prather?

DOROTHY

They're not cheap. I have catalogues from both of them. Would you like to take them home and look them over?
        (*She opens her briefcase.*)
I have them here.
        (*She hands them to* HORACE.)

HORACE

Thank you so much.

DOROTHY

You're welcome, Horace. Think carefully about all of this, Horace. You are talented certainly, but you are so very young.

HORACE

Yes, ma'am.

A section of the living room of the Robedaux house. There are an upright piano and several chairs. ELIZABETH, *thirty-five,* HORACE's *mother, is there playing "Narcissus" on the piano.* JIM, HORACE's *younger brother, nine, enters.*

JIM

Ma, can I go to the movies this afternoon?

> (*She continues playing, not paying any attention to him. He walks over to her and speaks in a very loud voice making himself heard over the piano.*)

Ma, can I go to the movies tonight? I've done all my homework.

ELIZABETH *stops playing and looks at him.*

ELIZABETH

May I go to the movies tonight?

JIM

May I? I've done all of my homework.

ELIZABETH

All of it?

JIM

Every single bit of it.

ELIZABETH

What's playing?

JIM

I don't know. It's a talking picture, I know that much.

ELIZABETH

Aren't they all talking pictures these days?

JIM

No, ma'am. Some are just part talking and on Saturdays the
serials are all silent.

ELIZABETH

Well, call the theater and see what's playing.

JIM

I've done all my homework.

ELIZABETH

That's all well and good, but I still don't want you to go and
see just any talking picture. Some pictures are not suitable, in
my opinion, for children.

He goes. She continues playing "Narcissus." JIM *comes back.*

JIM

Mama.
        (*She continues playing.*)
Mama?

ELIZABETH

        (*As she continues playing*)
Yes?

JIM

I know the name of the picture.

ELIZABETH

        (*She continues playing.*)
What?

JIM

Weary River.

ELIZABETH

Weary River? What's that about?

JIM

I don't know. They said it was a love story.

ELIZABETH

A what?

JIM

A love story.

ELIZABETH

Did they say it was suitable for children?

JIM

I don't know. I didn't ask.

ELIZABETH

Who's in it?

JIM

Lila Lee, Betty Compson, and Richard Barthelmes.

ELIZABETH

I don't think so.

JIM

Mom.

ELIZABETH

No, Jim. It all sounds too adult to me. Anyway, movies are expensive. You just can't go to the movies every time you turn around.

JIM

You let Horace go to the tent show every night when it's in town.

ELIZABETH

But that's only for a week. Anyway, Mr. Dude Arthur always trades at your daddy's store while he's in town. You could go to the tent show every night if you wanted to.

JIM

I don't like tent shows. I like the movies. The movies only cost a dime for children.

ELIZABETH

Only a dime. Dimes don't grow on trees, you know.
(HORACE *enters. He has school books.*)
Hello, Son.

HORACE

Hello.

ELIZABETH

How was school?

HORACE

Okay. Miss Prather gave me a copy of the senior play she's doing.

JIM

Are you going to be in it?

HORACE

Yes.

JIM

Are you going to play the lead?

HORACE

I don't know.

JIM

I bet you do. All the kids say Miss Prather thinks you hung the moon.

HORACE

I'm going to go read the play.

ELIZABETH

Do you have homework?

HORACE

Not much.

He goes. She continues playing.

JIM

I wonder if this one is going to be about a dope fiend too. Kids that saw the play in San Antonio said when he told roommates he was a dope fiend and needed dope right at that moment he began to tremble and shake. They thought he was going to have a fit. I wish I could have seen it.

HORACE SENIOR *comes in.*

HORACE SENIOR

Hello.

ELIZABETH

You're early.

HORACE SENIOR

I know.
(*He kisses her on the cheek.*)
Run on, Jim.

JIM

Why?

HORACE SENIOR

I want to talk to your mother about something.

JIM

About what?

HORACE SENIOR

Never mind about what. Just leave us alone for a while.
(*He goes.*)
Where's Horace?

ELIZABETH

He's in his room.

HORACE SENIOR

Studying?

ELIZABETH

I don't think so. Miss Prather gave him a copy today of the play they're doing as the senior play.

HORACE SENIOR

Elizabeth, as you know I've always felt leaving school as I had to do in the sixth grade in order to go to work to support myself was a great disadvantage to me. I've always felt if I had only had a proper education, finished high school, gone to college—
(*A pause*)

Well, I wouldn't always feel such a terrible failure. I haven't
accomplished much, you know.

ELIZABETH
I don't agree. I think on the contrary you have managed very
well in these terrible times. We have all the food we need, we
have the clothes we need, and we have this house.

HORACE SENIOR
Which your Papa gave us.

ELIZABETH
Never mind. We've never had to mortgage it. We—

HORACE SENIOR
I get no credit for that. I couldn't mortgage it even if I wanted
to. You are not allowed to mortgage your homestead in the
state of Texas. It's against the law. Anyway, it's not about me.
It's about Horace Junior. I've been thinking more and more
this last week about his graduation. Do you realize he'll be
graduating in two months?

ELIZABETH
I know. Is it possible?

HORACE SENIOR
I was thinking all day yesterday and last night and again today,
what would I most want to change about my life? And, of
course, I would like to have been able to finish high school
and go to college and get a profession like law or medicine or
engineering, but I was never good in math, so I probably
couldn't have been an engineer. Anyway, something to give me
a proper education so I'd be equipped to do more than run a
store. All that's too late for me now, of course, but I remember so well when Horace Junior was born I made a promise
to myself I was going to see when he grew up he was going to
have all the advantages my mama couldn't give me. I thought
today that's all well and good to remember promises, but what
can I do about the promises? I can barely keep the store afloat
these days, as you know. I've had to go to the bank twice and
borrow money to pay current bills. I tell you I felt so sad and

blue, and I thought where in the world can I turn now? When Mr. Beard came into the store I thought, it's not the first of the month, why is he here to pay his rent? And so I said, "You're early. Your rent's not due for another week." And then I thought to myself something about the house needs fixing and he's here to get me to have it done, and I asked him if that's why he was here or was he here to pay his rent early. "No," he said, "I'm not here for either reason, but to talk to you about some business." "What kind of business?" I said. "Have you ever thought about selling your rent house?" he asked. "No, I haven't," I said. "You bought it from your father-in-law didn't you?" he said. "Yes," I said, "in 1918. Cotton was selling for forty cents a pound and the war was on and every-body had a little money then." "Do you remember what you paid for it?" "Yes." "Well, would you be willing to sell it to me now if you made a profit?" "Well, I'd certainly think about it. I have to talk it over with my wife first, of course." "I under-stand," he said. "I'll pay you three thousand dollars for the house." "Yes, sir," I said. "Let me talk to my wife." And that's a thousand dollar profit, you know, hon. And I figure the three thousand dollars will get Horace Junior into not a fancy col-lege maybe, but a good one, and it will see him through four years. Of course he won't be able to join a fraternity and he'll have to come back here and work with me in the store during summer vacations.

(*A pause*)
What do you think?

ELIZABETH

Well—

HORACE SENIOR

I think it's a miracle, honey. The rent house is old and needs repairs. I've never been able to rent it for more than twenty dollars a month—

ELIZABETH

Well, it's certainly alright with me. I'm sure Horace Junior will just be delighted.

HORACE SENIOR

Without saying anything about it, I've been sending off for catalogues of schools I knew were reasonable. I have some down
at the store he can look at tonight.

(JIM *enters.*)

Where's Horace?

JIM

He's in his room.

ELIZABETH

What's he doing?

JIM

He's muttering to himself. I think he's reading aloud about
that play they're doing.

HORACE SENIOR

Go tell him to come here.

JIM

Yes, sir.

He goes.

HORACE SENIOR

Shall I tell him or you?

ELIZABETH

You tell him.

HORACE *enters.*

HORACE SENIOR

Horace?

HORACE

Yes, sir.

HORACE SENIOR

Sit down, Son.

HORACE

Yes, sir.

(*A pause*)

HORACE SENIOR

Son, you know our rent house the Beards are renting?

HORACE

Yes, sir.

HORACE SENIOR

I'm going to sell it.

HORACE

To whom?

HORACE SENIOR

Mr. Beard. He came to the store today and offered to buy it.

HORACE

Do you want to sell it, Daddy?

HORACE SENIOR

Yes, I do. It's run down, you know, and I'll never be able to get much rent the state it's in.
(*A pause*)
You know why I'm so happy I can sell it?

HORACE

No, sir.

HORACE SENIOR

So I can do for you what my mama couldn't ever do for me.

HORACE

What's that, Daddy?

HORACE SENIOR

Send you to college. Of course it will have to be a state school. And you won't be able to join a fraternity or anything fancy like that. I have been figuring ever since talking to Mr. Beard and I can just about manage four years for what I'll get for the house.

HORACE

What are you selling it for?

HORACE SENIOR

Three thousand dollars.

ELIZABETH

Isn't it wonderful, Horace?

HORACE

Yes, ma'am.

HORACE SENIOR

And I have a lot of college catalogues at the store we could look over together and after supper I'll go down and get them and bring them back here.

HORACE

Yes, sir.

Horace Senior looks at his watch.

HORACE SENIOR

What time is supper, Elizabeth?

ELIZABETH

In another hour.

HORACE SENIOR

I tell you what. I think I'll go down now and get those catalogues and we can begin looking at them before supper.

HORACE

Yes, sir.
    (A pause)
Daddy?

HORACE SENIOR

Yes, Son.

HORACE

I feel terrible about this, but I have to tell you something.

HORACE SENIOR

Tell me what, Son?

HORACE

I don't want to go to college.

HORACE SENIOR

What?

HORACE

I don't want to go to college.

HORACE SENIOR

You have to go to college, Son. You'll regret it the rest of
your life if you don't go to college. If you go to college you'll
have all kinds of opportunities I never had. I want you to go
to college.

HORACE

I don't want to go to college, Dad.

ELIZABETH

Why not, Son?

HORACE

I don't know how to tell you, but I just don't.

HORACE SENIOR

You can tell me, Son. I'm your father. Don't be afraid. I'll understand. Whatever it is.

HORACE

Yes, sir. I hope so.
     (*A pause*)
I don't want to go to college, because I want to be an actor—

HORACE SENIOR

Good God Almighty! Did you hear that, Elizabeth? Am I
dreaming, or did he say what I think he did. What did he say,
Elizabeth?

ELIZABETH

You heard him correctly. He said he doesn't want to go to college, because he wants to be an actor.

HORACE SENIOR

An actor! An actor! What kind of an actor? Like Wallace Reid
who died a dope fiend? Like Fatty Arbuckle arrested in a sex
scandal? Like Charlie Chaplain seducing young innocent girls?
Or maybe like Dude Arthur, with his tent show, half drunk all
the time. Talk to him about the life of an actor. You know what

he told me? He said he'd rather a child of his would take a
pistol and blow his brains out than be an actor.

ELIZABETH

Come on, honey. Just calm down now.

HORACE SENIOR

Where do such ideas come from? Where did he get such an
idea here in Harrison, Texas? Did your teacher put all this in
your head? Has she put you up to all this? What is the new
play you're in about? More dope fiends?

HORACE

No, sir. It's a period piece about life in New York City. Eva Le
Gallienne played in it in New York.

HORACE SENIOR

Who in the world is that?

HORACE

I don't really know, sir. I only know what Miss Prather told me.
She said she is a great actress. She was in Lilliom in New York
City.

HORACE SENIOR

In what?

HORACE

Lilliom.

HORACE SENIOR

What's that?

HORACE

What's what?

HORACE SENIOR

Lilliom or whatever you said.

HORACE

That was a play in New York.

HORACE SENIOR

Is that about dope too?

HORACE

No, sir. I don't think so. I don't know what it's about.

HORACE SENIOR

Well, where did all this foolishness come from if not from that
teacher of yours?

HORACE

Do you remember old Mr. Armstrong?

HORACE SENIOR

Yes.

HORACE

And you used to tell me he had a call to come to Texas to preach?

HORACE SENIOR

Yes.

HORACE

Well, one day I had a call just—

HORACE SENIOR

You had a what?

HORACE

A call.

HORACE SENIOR

What kind of a call?

HORACE

It's hard to describe, Daddy. It's just like something came to
me and said you want to be an actor.

HORACE SENIOR

I never heard of such a thing. Did it say aloud, "You want to
be an actor"?

HORACE

No, sir, not really, but I heard it.

HORACE SENIOR

I understand you heard it, but was it a man's voice or a
woman's voice?

HORACE

No, sir. Come to think of it. It was more like a feeling, like—

HORACE SENIOR

Like what?

HORACE

I don't know, sir. It was like nothing I have ever experienced before, or since.

HORACE SENIOR

God Almighty. I never heard of such a thing.
(*A pause*)
Well, what did you do after this whatever it was spoke to you?

HORACE

I went to Mother and I asked what Mr. Armstrong did after he got his call, and Mother said he probably prayed and asked God to tell him what to do. So I prayed and asked God to tell me what to do.

HORACE SENIOR

How long ago was this?

HORACE

About a year and a half ago.

HORACE SENIOR

Why didn't you tell your mother and me about it?

HORACE

I thought you'd make fun of me, and tell me I was foolish and crazy. Then, soon after, Miss Prather came here to teach and began to put on plays, and I thought maybe God sent her to help me be an actor, and I prayed some more.

ELIZABETH

How did you pray, Son?

HORACE

I just prayed. I prayed to know if I should tell Miss Prather that I wanted to be an actor. But I was afraid to just then, so I didn't. But it came to me to write Mr. Dude Arthur to see if

I could see him next time he was in Harrison and ask him how I could go about being an actor. I wrote him, but he never answered. The next time his show was in town I went by his boardinghouse and he was there, but he was drunk. I decided not to ask him anything then and started to leave, but he kept asking me why I had come there. I finally said I had written him a letter and sent it to Tyler, Texas, and had he gotten it. He said no and what was the letter about. I said I wanted advice on how to become an actor. He said why in the name of God. I said because I wanted to know as I wanted to spend my life when I got out of high school acting. He said, well, you're a fool and get over it. Mrs. Arthur came in then and she yelled at him and said he'd better start sobering up as he had a show that night. I left and the next day while I was at the store with Daddy, he came in and he told Daddy about my visit to him and that I said I wanted to be an actor. After he left, Daddy yelled at me and said he'd never heard of such a thing and to get over it.

ELIZABETH

Is that right, Horace?

HORACE SENIOR

Yes, it is.

ELIZABETH

You never told me about it.

HORACE SENIOR

I didn't see any use in worrying you, as I knew he'd get over it. You remember George Rust said he wanted to be a painter, and his family sent him east to study and after two years he came back here and built him a studio so he could spend his time painting and it lasted about six months and then he got tired of it so he ended up managing his family's cotton farm.

HORACE

Anyway, since Daddy was so opposed to it and Mr. Arthur wasn't at all encouraging, I decided maybe God hadn't spoken to me after all, and I wasn't going to be an actor. But then Mother asked if I wanted to go and see the Ben Greet Play-

ers. I said yes, and when I got to the theater where they were
playing, I looked across the street where Florence Reed was
playing and something told me to go there instead of to the
Ben Greet Players. So I went to that instead of the Ben Greet
Players and when the play was over I knew I had to be an
actor for sure now, and I told Miss Prather what I wanted to
do today. She wasn't as encouraging as I thought she would
surely be, but she said if that's what I wanted to do, I should
go to school.

ELIZABETH

What kind of school, honey?

HORACE

A theater school's where they teach acting.

ELIZABETH

Are there such things? I didn't know that.

HORACE

Yes, ma'am. And she had sent away for catalogues for a school
in Pasadena and in New York City, which is the one I like the
best.

ELIZABETH

Why, honey?

HORACE

Because that's where Broadway is and they have lots of the-
aters there and—

HORACE SENIOR

Well, I'll tell you this. As sure as I'm standing here, you'll get
over it. Mr. Armstrong got over his call. He only preached for
five years and when he saw he couldn't half feed his family on
a preacher's salary, he began to sell insurance.
    (*A pause*)

HORACE

Dad?

HORACE SENIOR

Yes?

HORACE

I have some catalogues in my room from acting schools. Would you look at them?

HORACE SENIOR

No. It's all a lot of foolishness.

HORACE

Daddy?

HORACE SENIOR

Yes?

HORACE

Help me, Daddy. I'll never ask you for anything again in my life, but just help me and send me someplace where I can learn to be an actor. I'll never ask you for anything else ever again. I swear.

(*He begins to cry.*)

I swear. I know it's crazy, Daddy. I don't expect you and Mother to understand, but—

(*He's sobbing now. He controls himself.*)

I'm sorry. I'm sorry.

He leaves his parents disturbed and troubled by his crying. There is silence for a moment.

HORACE SENIOR

Well—

JIM *comes in.*

JIM

What's the matter with Horace?

ELIZABETH

Never mind. We'll talk about it later.

JIM

He was crying.

ELIZABETH

We're aware of it.

JIM

I never saw him cry before. He's sixteen. He shouldn't be crying at sixteen.

ELIZABETH

He's not sixteen yet.

JIM

He will be in March.

ELIZABETH

It isn't March yet.

HORACE SENIOR

Go ask Horace Junior to give you the catalogues of the schools
he was telling me about, and bring them to me.

JIM

What schools?

HORACE SENIOR

I don't know the names of them. He'll know what I'm talking
about.
    (JIM *goes.*)
When I was in the bank I saw Louie Worthing. He's pros-
pered, you know.

ELIZABETH

I know he has.

HORACE SENIOR

Made good investments.

ELIZABETH

I know.

HORACE SENIOR

He said he was investing in an oil pool, and that there was just one
share left, and he didn't want to influence me, one way or the
other, but he's investing in the oil pool, and he thinks whoever
invests in the pool can make quite a profit from their investment.

ELIZABETH

How much does the share cost?

HORACE SENIOR

Three thousand dollars, and I was tempted to invest the

money I will get from Mr. Beard, but I said to myself, if I lose the money, there goes Horace's college money.

JIM *comes in with two catalogues.* HORACE SENIOR *takes the catalogues and looks at them.* JIM *goes to the radio, turns it on, and looks for a program with music. The phone rings in another part of the house.* HORACE SENIOR *goes to answer it.* JIM *finds a station with popular music.*

ELIZABETH

Would you mind not playing that music now, Jim.
(*He looks around at her.*)
Just turn the radio off, please, Jim.

JIM

Why is everybody so upset?

HORACE SENIOR *comes back in and picks up the catalogues he had been looking at.*

ELIZABETH

Who was on the phone?

HORACE SENIOR

Louie Worthing. He says there is someone interested in that last share in the oil pool. He will have to give them an answer by nine tonight. He said he wanted me to understand he's putting no pressure on me, but he just thought I should know and I would have to decide before nine tonight.

He looks at his watch.

ELIZABETH

What time is it, Horace?

HORACE SENIOR

Seven.
(*A pause*)
Of course if Horace refuses to go to college I don't need the three thousand dollars right now. And if they strike oil as Louie believes they will, our whole life could turn around. What should I do, Elizabeth?

ELIZABETH

I don't know.

HORACE SENIOR

Of course I won't need money for Jim's college for another seven years. That is if he wants to go to college.

(*To Jim*)

I hope you don't wind up wanting to be an actor like your brother.

JIM

No, sir. I'd like to be a crooner, but I know I can't be, because I can't carry a tune unless I'm singing along with somebody.

HORACE SENIOR

Thank God for small favors.

(*A pause*)

I'm going to call Louie and tell him he can count me in on the pool.

(*He starts out of the room. He stops, thinking. He comes back into the room.*)

I can't do it. As sure as I invest in that oil well and lose my money, Horace will come to me and say, "I've changed my mind and I want to go to college."

A pause. He picks up the catalogues and looks at them.

JIM

Horace told me just now he'll never go to college. That he's going to be an actor. He says he had a call.

HORACE SENIOR

I know all about that call business.

ELIZABETH

If he goes to acting school Pasadena is cheaper than New York.

HORACE SENIOR

I'll never help him to get to New York to school. Not a fifteen-year-old boy.

JIM

He's almost sixteen.

HORACE SENIOR

You keep out of it, Jim. How much is Pasadena?

ELIZABETH

It's a two-year course. Seven hundred and fifty dollars for the first year and two hundred and fifty dollars for the second. Mama has two sisters out in California. Aunt Mag and Aunt Bobo.

HORACE SENIOR

I remember.

ELIZABETH

A thousand dollars for two years. That will still leave you two thousand dollars.

HORACE SENIOR

Not really. Does the thousand include board and room?

ELIZABETH

No, I guess not.

HORACE SENIOR

And there is the fare to California and back.

ELIZABETH

He could take the bus.

HORACE SENIOR

Even the bus costs money, Elizabeth. You see it all adds up.
(A pause)
And what worries me the most is does a fifteen-year-old boy really know what he wants to do? What if we send him out there and he doesn't like it and wants to go to college? What then?

ELIZABETH

I don't know what then. I'm no fortune-teller.
(A pause)
He was very upset, I only know that. I've never seen him so upset. Have you?

HORACE SENIOR

No.
(A pause)

Here's what I think we should do. Make a bargain with him.
Let him stay here next year after he graduates and work with
me in the store, and if at the end of the year he still wants to
go to acting school, we'll send him to Pasadena. Does that
seem sensible to you?

ELIZABETH

Yes, it does. It sounds very sensible to me.

HORACE SENIOR

Of course, I think he'll change his mind while he waits out the
year. He'll realize how chancy this whole acting business is and
come to his senses and say, "I was wrong, I want to go to college." In the meantime I'll leave all the college catalogues I
sent for around the living room so he can see them and look
at them if he wants to.
　　(*Calling*)
Horace Junior.

HORACE

　　(*Calling offstage*)
Yes, sir.

HORACE SENIOR

Can you come here please.

*Horace Senior goes back to looking at the catalogues he has. Horace Ju-
nior enters.*

HORACE

Yes, sir.

HORACE SENIOR

Sit down, Son.

HORACE

Yes, sir.

HORACE SENIOR

We've been looking over the catalogues.

HORACE

Yes, sir.

HORACE SENIOR

Does either of these schools guarantee you a job when you finish their curriculum?

HORACE

I don't believe so, sir.

JIM

No college guarantees you a job, Daddy.

HORACE SENIOR

You keep out of this, Jim, or I'll send you to your room.

JIM

Yes, sir.

HORACE SENIOR

You see, I don't want you to think your daddy doesn't want to help you in any way I can, but we just want to be sure it's what you really want to do.

HORACE

I understand, Papa.

HORACE SENIOR

You know Mr. George Rust?

HORACE

Yes, sir.

HORACE SENIOR

Well, when he was seventeen and graduated from high school he said he wanted to be a painter.

JIM

What kind of painter? A house painter?

HORACE SENIOR

No, not a house painter, Jim. An artist. He wanted to paint pictures of people and houses and cotton fields and God knows what all. That's all he would do from morning until night, and he got his family to send him east so he could study painting and off he went and stayed away for two years and

studied painting and came back here and his family built him
a studio and he painted night and day and then he got tired of
it and quit and he's never painted a day since and manages his
family's cotton farms.

HORACE

You told me about that earlier, Daddy.

HORACE SENIOR

Oh, did I? I guess I did.

ELIZABETH

And I had a cousin in Brazoria who was bound and deter-
mined to be an artist of some kind, and her family sent her to
live in Greenwich Village where she could be an artist. She
even got into O. O. McIntyre's column in New York about
something she did in Greenwich Village like squirting some
red ink on the monument in Washington Square or something
like that, and then she lost her mind, the poor thing, and they
had to bring her back home and she wound up in the asylum.

HORACE

I'm not going to lose my mind, Mama. I'm going to work hard
and make a success.

ELIZABETH

I'm sure you will, darling, but I just want you to know why we
worry.

HORACE SENIOR
(*Glancing at the Playhouse brochure*)
Who is Gilmore Brown?

HORACE

It says there he's the head of the Playhouse. The artistic director.

HORACE SENIOR

I see. And who is Charles Prickett?

HORACE

According to the brochure he's the business manager.
(*A pause*)

HORACE SENIOR

Well, I'll make a bargain with you. Wait a year until you're seventeen and work in the store with me in the meantime. If at the end of the year you still want to study acting, I'll help you go to Pasadena.

Horace is moved and relieved by their decision, but controls his emotions.

HORACE

Yes, sir. Thank you, sir. I appreciate it.

He goes.

HORACE SENIOR

Well, I bet you anything I have he'll come to his senses after a month or two here working in the store and he'll say, "I've changed my mind. I want to go to college."

(*A pause*)

Do I have time to work in the garden a little before supper?

ELIZABETH

Yes, you do.

JIM

What are we having?

ELIZABETH

Nothing special. A casserole. Horace, what if he doesn't change his mind?

HORACE SENIOR

Then I don't know.

He goes.

ELIZABETH

Jim, in about half an hour set the table for me, will you?

JIM

Yes, ma'am.

(*She goes. He picks up the Pasadena brochure and looks at it.* HORACE *comes in.*)

Who are Onshlow Stevens and Gloria Stewart?

HORACE

Why?

JIM

It says here they are movie stars and went to the Pasadena Playhouse and were discovered there by Hollywood. Did you ever hear of them?

HORACE

Yes, I did.

JIM

Well I haven't. And Victor Jory. Did you ever hear of him?

HORACE

Yes, I did.

JIM

Are you calmer now?

HORACE

Yes, I am.

(ELIZABETH *enters.* HORACE *takes the Pasadena brochure and starts to look at it. He begins to sing to himself.*)
"Once I built a railroad,
Made it run,
Made it race against time.
Once I built a railroad,
Now it's done,
Brother, can you spare a dime?"

ELIZABETH

Horace?

HORACE

Yes, ma'am.

ELIZABETH

Would you mind not singing that song around your father. He finds it depressing.

HORACE

Yes, ma'am.
(*He puts the brochure down.* JIM *picks it up and begins reading it.* ELIZABETH *takes the American*

Academy brochure and begins to read that. HORACE
*walks to the front of the stage and addresses the
audience.)*

My father asked me not to tell anyone in town that he was
thinking of sending me to dramatic school until it was time for
me to go. Jim said he kept hoping I'd change my mind and ask
to go to college. At first he left college catalogues all over the
house. But when he saw I wasn't going to change my mind
they began to disappear. A lot of my friends went off to college, those that didn't mostly went to Houston looking for
jobs. Dude Arthur's tent show came for one last summer and
then it closed down for good. They did a show in Harrison
called a "Womanless Wedding" with men from town playing
all the parts. Dearie Burtner, who was big and fat and had
been my scout master when I was in Cub Scouts, was the
bride and Mr. Piney, who was thin as a rake and only came up
to Dearie's shoulders, was the groom. They asked me to be
in it, but I declined. People in town said that was the kind
of show they liked. Clean, wholesome, and fun. Vilma Banky
and Rod LaRocque, two movie stars that couldn't get work
because of their accents when talkies began, came to Houston
in a play called Cherries Are Ripe. I went to see it, but I didn't
like it. The well Louie Worthing's pool invested in came
through and Louie Worthing and all his investors became rich.
Some said they made as much as fifty thousand apiece. Anyway, the ones I knew all got new cars for themselves and their
wives and children. It wasn't until years later my mother told
me Daddy could have been one of the investors, but was
afraid they would find no oil and the three thousand dollars he
had for me would be lost. When news got around town that
my folks were sending me off to dramatic school, my daddy
had many visitors. Mostly old men, he said, came to the store
to tell him he was making a mistake and just throwing his
money away. Most of them, he said, used George Rust as an
example of how it would finally turn out. I was in the store
when the last one came in. An uncle on Daddy's side. I was in
the front of the store and Daddy was in the back at his desk
working on his accounts when this uncle came in. He barely

spoke to me and asked where Daddy was and I pointed to the
back of the store, and I called out, "Daddy, Uncle Albert is
here to see you." He went on towards Daddy in the back of
the store. I could hear him say he was here as a concerned
member of the family to try and talk some sense into Daddy.
I heard Daddy say he would thank him to mind his own business. Then his uncle brought up George Rust one more time
and they began to yell at each other over that and his uncle
left in a fury without saying goodbye to Daddy or me. The
night I was to leave for California he and Mother went to sit
on the gallery after supper. I was in my room packing my suit-
case while listening to the radio, when Daddy called and asked
me to come out on the porch. I went out and there was a
moon, partly obscured by a cloud, but high in the sky. Daddy
gave me my bus ticket and told me to be careful of pickpock-
ets, and I said I would. He gave me a twenty dollar bill then,
which he said I should save in case an emergency of some kind
came up. I thanked him and Mother began crying then and
said they were going to miss me. I said I would miss them too.
Daddy said they were both very proud of me and felt I would
have a wonderful success, but to always remember that if
things didn't work out in California or any other place, I could
always come back to my home and be welcomed and there
would be a place for me to work in his store. I thanked him
for telling me that. I never did go back during their lifetime
except on visits, though many a time when I was lonely and
discouraged I wanted to. But then I remembered about my
call and kept on going somehow.

The lights fade.

OUTSTANDING DRAMA FROM THE OVERLOOK PRESS

Edward Albee, THE GOAT
1-58567-364-1 *Cloth* $22.95

Edward Albee, THE PLAY ABOUT THE BABY
1-58567-353-6 *Cloth* $22.95

Horton Foote, THE LAST OF THE THORNTONS (*Sewanee Writers' Series*)
1-58567-048-0 *Paper* $12.95

Richard Foreman, MY HEAD WAS A SLEDGEHAMMER *Six Plays*
0-87951-575-9 *Cloth* $35.00, 0-87951-622-4 *Paper* $19.95

Richard Foreman, PARADISE HOTEL *and Other Plays*
1-58567-004-9 *Cloth* $29.95, 1-58567-015-4 *Paper* $19.95

John Guare, THE HOUSE OF BLUE LEAVES *and* CHAUCER IN ROME *Two Plays*
1-58567-291-2 *Paper* $17.95

John Guare, LYDIE BREEZE
1-58567-158-4 *Paper* $16.95

Arthur Kopit, Y2K
1-58567-025-1 *Paper* $11.95

Naomi Iizuka, 36 VIEWS
1-58567-383-8 *Paper* $14.95

Neil LaBute, BASH *Three Plays*
1-58567-024-3 *Paper* $14.95

Neil LaBute, THE DISTANCE FROM HERE
1-58567-371-4 *Paper* $14.95

David Lindsay-Abaire, FUDDY MEERS
1-58567-122-3 *Paper* $14.95

David Lindsay-Abaire, WONDER OF THE WORLD
1-58567-311-0 *Paper* $14.95

John Logan, NEVER THE SINNER
0-87951-930-4 *Paper* $12.95

Kenneth Lonergan, THIS IS OUR YOUTH
1-58567-018-9 *Paper* $14.95

John Cameron Mitchell, HEDWIG AND THE ANGRY INCH
Music and Lyrics by Stephen Trask
1-58567-034-0 *Cloth* $24.95, 1-58567-295-5 *Paper* $16.95

Paul Rudnick, THE MOST FABULOUS STORY EVER TOLD
and MR. CHARLES, CURRENTLY OF PALM BEACH *Two Plays*
1-58567-052-9 *Paper* $14.95

Diana Son, STOP KISS
0-87951-737-9 *Paper* $14.95

August Wilson, JITNEY
1-58567-186-X *Cloth* $22.95; 1-58567-370-6 *Paper* $14.95

THE OVERLOOK PRESS
WOODSTOCK & NEW YORK
www.overlookpress.com